A Child's First Library of Learning

Geography

TIME-LIFE BOOKS • ALEXANDRIA, VIRGINIA

Contents

❓ How Are Maps Made?

ANSWER A map shows at a glance how far one place is from another and how to travel to the next town or around the world. Maps also indicate the size of a town, the height of a mountain, and the depth of an ocean. In the past surveyors made detailed measurements by hand to determine the size and shape of the land and the distance between any two points. Today airplanes and satellites survey the earth with instruments and make fast and accurate calculations from which maps are drawn.

■ Map making

1 When mapmakers decide on the area to be drawn, surveyors determine its measurements. The surveying equipment and instruments shown here include the hand-held level at left and the telescope on a tripod at right. The instruments measure angles and determine distance, elevation—or height—and direction.

2 A plane *(left)* flies over the area determined in Step 1, and a photographer takes pictures of the town from directly overhead. For views of a larger area, mapmakers also use satellite photographs *(top)*.

3 A detailed survey follows. Features that do not show up in photographs are checked out on the ground *(right)*. That is the only way to determine boundaries between towns, the names of streets, or anything else that the camera does not see.

4 Based on the measurements and photographs, mapmakers draw a precise map and label the streets and important buildings.

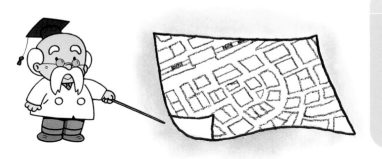

What Does a Bird's-Eye View of the North Pole Look Like?

ANSWER The North Pole is located on the part of the earth that is shown at the top of a world map or a globe. If you could look down on the North Pole like a bird flying overhead, the land and ocean would look different from what you see on a flat map, because the earth is round.

■ A map centered on the North Pole

You usually look at a globe from the side. Try looking at it from above.

North America

North Pole

Asia

If you looked down on the North Pole, you would see the earth as in the map at left. This kind of map shows the landmasses of North America, Europe, Asia, and even parts of Africa.

■ How to make this map

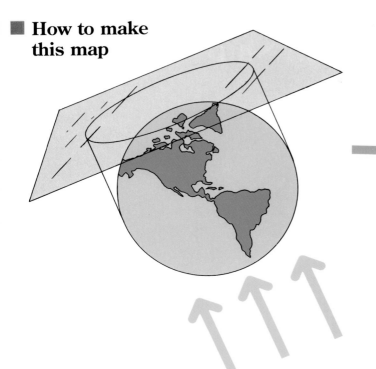

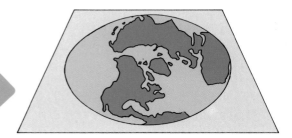

▲ You draw this map by beginning at the one point where the flat map touches the globe.

▲ If you laid a transparent sheet directly on the North Pole and traced what you saw, your map would look like the one above at right.

How about the South Pole?

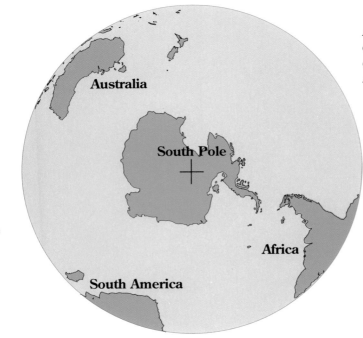

A map centered on the South Pole features the continent of Antarctica surrounded by ocean. The closest continents visible on this map are South America, Africa, and Australia.

Australia

South Pole

Africa

South America

● To the Parent

One problem with making maps is that the earth is round but a map is flat. Cartographers use mathematical formulas to project the earth's round surface on flat paper. One kind of projection, called azimuthal, allows cartographers to center the map on a certain point, such as the North Pole, to achieve the greatest accuracy at that point. Other methods for showing the round earth on a flat surface include cylindrical and conic projections. All of these maps use some method of projecting lines of latitude and longitude.

❓ What Maps Are Used on Ships?

ANSWER To find their way across the ocean, ships navigate by special maps known as charts. Charts show the depth of the water and any dangerous areas. One map used by sailors since 1569 is the Mercator projection, named after Flemish mapmaker Gerardus Mercator. On these maps sailors can plot a course as a straight line between any two points.

▶ Since maps for ships are used on the trackless sea, they must show bearings, the direction from one point to another as determined by a compass.

■ Mercator projection

On a Mercator map *(below)* many countries look distorted and stretched, especially on the upper and lower ends of the map. But a line drawn from any position to any destination will give the most direct course for a ship.

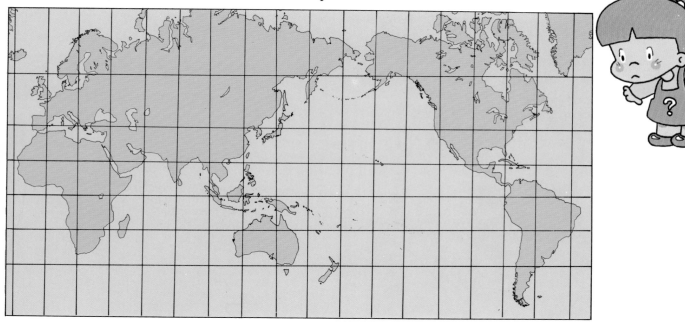

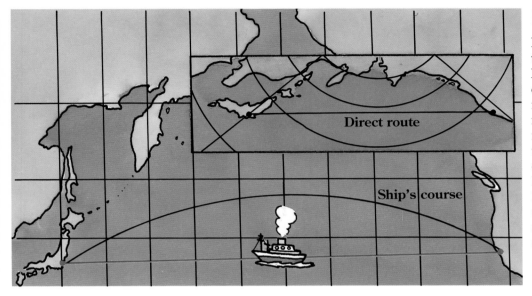

■ Ships' maps

If a ship sails on a course determined by a line on a Mercator map, it can reach its destination, although it may not have taken the shortest route. A straight line on the map *(straight line in inset)* is the most direct route. But because the earth is round the line represents a curved path. If the ship is traveling near the equator, a Mercator map will show the shortest route along a straight line.

■ How to find a course

On a ship, even though you know where on the map you want to go, you cannot tell which direction to take unless you know your own position. Ships constantly check their position by determining how long a radio signal takes to reach them from a shore station or a satellite.

▲**Signals from shore.** The length of time a radio signal takes to arrive from a station tells the crew how far the ship is from land.

◄**Signals from satellites.** Large ships can receive satellite signals that tell them their position and bearing.

Why Are Maps Rectangular When the Earth Is Round?

ANSWER The earth is a sphere and cannot be represented by a flat map without stretching and distorting parts of it. Many different maps have been developed to show the round earth on a flat surface, but the most convenient shape is rectangular.

■ Method 1

▲ Surround the globe with a cylinder.

▲ Trace the earth onto the cylinder.

▲ Flatten the cylinder, and you have a rectangular map.

MINI-DATA

In 1988 the National Geographic Society decided that the Robinson projection *(right)* would be the simplest map to use from the more than 200 projections available. The Robinson projection renders most countries accurate in size, outlining the countries in the midsection of the map with little distortion.

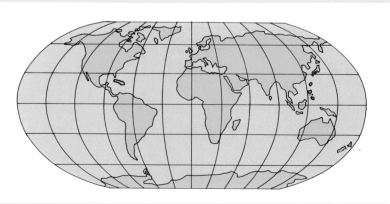

■ Method 2

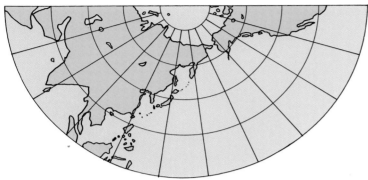

◁ Place a cone on a globe with its point directly above the North Pole and trace the earth on the cone. This kind of map, called a conic projection, is useful for mapping midsections of the globe.

▽ The map below was made by placing a cone on the South Pole.

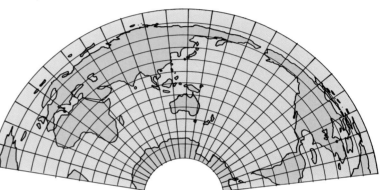

▲ The map above, called Goode's Interrupted, combines the advantages of conic and cylindrical maps by nearly representing the proper size of every continent. This map looks a little like the peel of an orange removed in a single piece.

11

How Are Mountains Shown on Maps?

ANSWER Mapmakers use contour lines to show how high mountains are. These lines connect points that are all at the same elevation, or height above sea level. In addition, bands of color help to point out each higher level.

■ From tall to flat

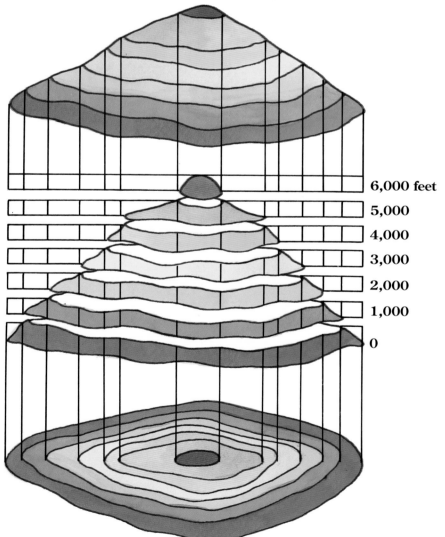

6,000 feet
5,000
4,000
3,000
2,000
1,000
0

The illustration at left shows a mountain from the side. Color bands and curving contour lines indicate different levels of elevation.

The same mountain is represented as a graph in separate bands of color.

All points of the same height are joined by a contour line. By using different colors for each level, mountains of any height can be illustrated clearly on a map.

■ From photo to map

Matsuda, a small mountain community in Japan, is shown in the aerial photo at right. A mapmaker converted the information in the photograph to draw the map below. Compare the map with the photograph, and see how many places you can identify. The dots inside triangles are bench marks, and the numbers beside them show the elevation. The number 300 on the contour line at top center indicates that every point on the line is 300 meters (985 feet) above sea level.

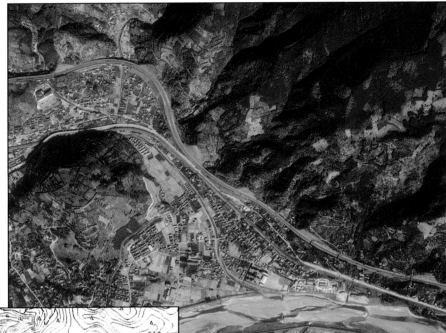

▲ **An aerial photograph**

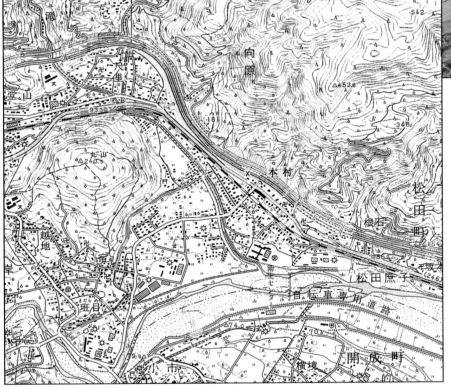

▲ **A map**

Can the Ocean Be Mapped?

ANSWER Oceans are not the same depth all over. Underneath the water lie mountains and valleys that look much like the surface of the land. Oceans are so deep that people cannot easily measure them or dive down to find the bottom. Scientists determine the depth instead with instruments from aboard ships. These instruments can find the depth at a certain point. Scientists must measure at thousands of points to map the ocean floor accurately.

■ Sounding the depth

One way to measure the depth of the ocean is by sound waves. Instruments on a ship send beams of sound waves through the water. The sound waves reflect off the ocean floor and return as echoes. Scientists calculate the depth by measuring the time it takes the sound waves to bounce back.

■ Sound reflection

■ The ocean floor

At one time people believed that the ocean floor was uniformly flat. Not until the 1920s did scientists begin to map the bottom of the ocean with sounding equipment. They found that oceans have valleys and mountains, plains and trenches, as shown in the illustration at right of the Pacific Ocean.

▲ Pacific Ocean

A chain of mountains runs through the center of the Atlantic Ocean, shown at left. The shallow areas appear in white and the deepest canyons in dark blue.

▲ Atlantic Ocean

● To the Parent

The ocean floor, like the surface of the land, has marked topographical features. In the maps at left and above, the floor of the Pacific Ocean shows towering rises and enormous trenches, some of them deeper than Mount Everest is high. An oceanic ridge runs north and south through the center of the Atlantic, but the rest of the seabed is more uniform. The differences in topography may be caused by convection currents in the mantle under the surface of the earth.

15

How Do You Measure a Mountain?

ANSWER If you had a long enough ruler you could measure the height of a mountain directly. Since such rulers don't exist, surveyors use different types of rulers and instruments to calculate the elevation of hills and mountains on the surface of the earth.

■ Measuring hills

1 Surveyors begin at a reference point with a known height. At that point and at the point to be measured, surveyors hold up long rods. Between those points stands a person with a measuring instrument called a transit.

5.0

2 The surveyor *(center at left and above)* looks through the transit at the leveling rods, held by the two helpers. From the numbers she reads off the rods, she can calculate the height of a particular point.

How Do You Measure Distance?

One way to measure distance is with a laser instrument that has a transmitter and a receiver. A surveyor sets up the instrument at one end of the distance to be measured and a reflector at the other end. When he transmits a beam of light, he measures the time it takes the beam to bounce back from the reflector to calculate the distance.

▶ To measure short distances, surveyors use 100-foot-long steel tapes.

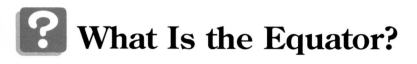

What Is the Equator?

ANSWER The equator is an imaginary line that encircles the globe at its widest part, halfway between the North Pole and the South Pole. This line divides the globe into Northern and Southern Hemispheres.

▶ The position of a particular point on earth is called *location*.

■ The equator

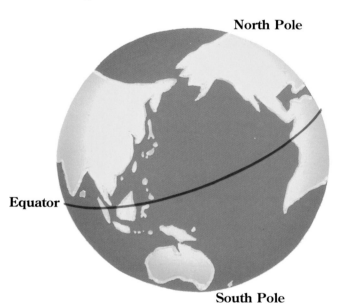

North Pole

Equator

South Pole

The red line shown on the globe in the illustration above is the equator. The equator is an imaginary line that everyone has agreed to; there is no actual line on the earth's surface.

■ Pinpointing a place

Mapmakers have divided maps and globes with additional lines that parallel the equator called lines of latitude.

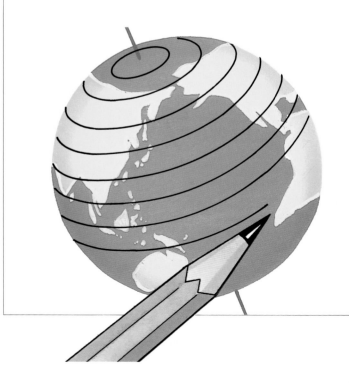

The prime meridian

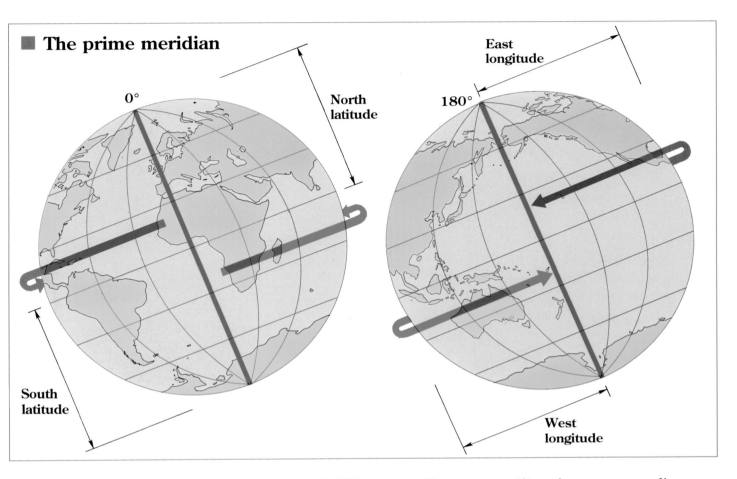

North latitude

South latitude

East longitude

West longitude

0°

180°

Vertical lines on a globe running from the North Pole to the South Pole are called lines of longitude. These lines cross with lines of latitude to form a grid and help pinpoint the location of any place on earth.

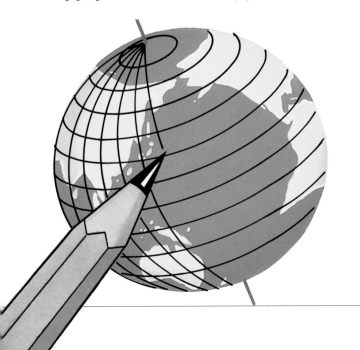

The prime meridian, shown as a green line on the globe above left, is the line of 0° longitude, the starting point for measuring distances east and west around the globe. Halfway around the globe lies the 180th meridian *(green line above)*. Roughly following this line is the International Date Line, the line from which the calendar days begin. When people cross the date line, they begin a new day. The prime meridian and the 180th meridian divide the globe into Eastern and Western Hemispheres.

Why Is It Always Hot near the Equator?

(ANSWER) In countries near the equator it is usually hot all year long except for a few areas in the high mountains. Equatorial countries receive the sun's hot rays more directly than countries farther to the north and south of the equator.

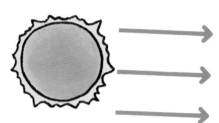

▲ As the earth revolves around the sun, it is tilted at 23.5°. This tilt affects the angle at which the sun's rays strike the ground in different parts of the world.

■ Near the equator

In places near the equator the sun's rays strike from directly overhead. The more direct sunlight causes higher temperatures that change little during the year.

■ Beyond the equator

Countries farther north of the equator, like the United States, Korea, Japan, and Europe, have four seasons. The way the earth tilts as it orbits the sun causes the sun's rays to strike various places at different angles depending on the time of year.

CHECK IT OUT

Fill two boxes of equal size with sand. Place them in the sun, one box flat on the ground, the other one at an angle. Put a thermometer in each box. You will see that the temperature rises faster in the box sitting flat on the ground, receiving the sun's rays straight on.

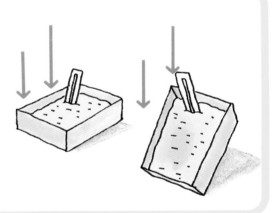

■ Far from the equator

In the icebound Antarctic the rays of the sun strike the earth at a very low angle. This angle transmits very little heat. What makes it even colder is that the ice acts the same way as a giant mirror, reflecting the sun's light and heat back into space so that the average temperature is -60° F.

Why Do Countries Have Borders?

ANSWER The boundaries between countries are called borders. These are dividing lines created by governments to separate one country from another. Sometimes borders run along natural features, such as rivers or mountain chains. But the most common borders are fences or stone markers.

▲ U.S.-Canadian border

■ Types of borders

In some countries borders are simply marked by flags, as at the crossing point between Canada and the United States *(top, right)*. When a frontier is defined by a river, the two countries are separated in the middle of the stream. If mountains divide two countries, the border follows the mountains' crest.

▲ A mountain range as border

▲ A river dividing two countries

▲ The ocean as natural border

22

■ Changing frontiers

Europe 1923

▲ The map above shows the borders of Europe in the early 1920s, after World War I. The map below displays the same area in 1945 after World War II, when some borders had changed. A few countries lost territory, while others gained some.

▼ **Europe 1945**

●To the Parent

Borders shift depending on the world situation. In the early 1990s, in response to ideological changes, the frontiers of East and West Germany, the former Soviet Union, and much of Eastern Europe were revised. Wars are the major cause of changing frontiers. The victor seizes territory from the loser. The maps of Europe at left and above show how some of the borders, and often the names as well, have changed in this century.

? What Is a Capital?

■ A capital's function

▼ The capital is a country's seat of government, where offices to conduct official business are located. It is often the largest and most important city in a country.

▲ High-rise buildings mark the center of Tokyo, the capital city of Japan *(above)*. The illustration at left shows the chambers of Japan's legislative body.

ANSWER The capital of a country is the city where the government meets to make the laws and enforce them. The country's ruler, whether a president, a prime minister, or a king, and other officials make decisions in the capital.

■ World capitals

▲ The capital of the United States is Washington, D.C., where Congress meets in the Capitol *(above).*

▶ Tokyo, Japan's capital *(right),* has a new city hall in a section of high-rise buildings called Shinjuku.

◀ Paris *(left),* the capital of France, can be identified by its central arch, the Arc de Triomphe, in a city world famous for the arts, fashion, and good food.

? Can You Name the Fifty States?

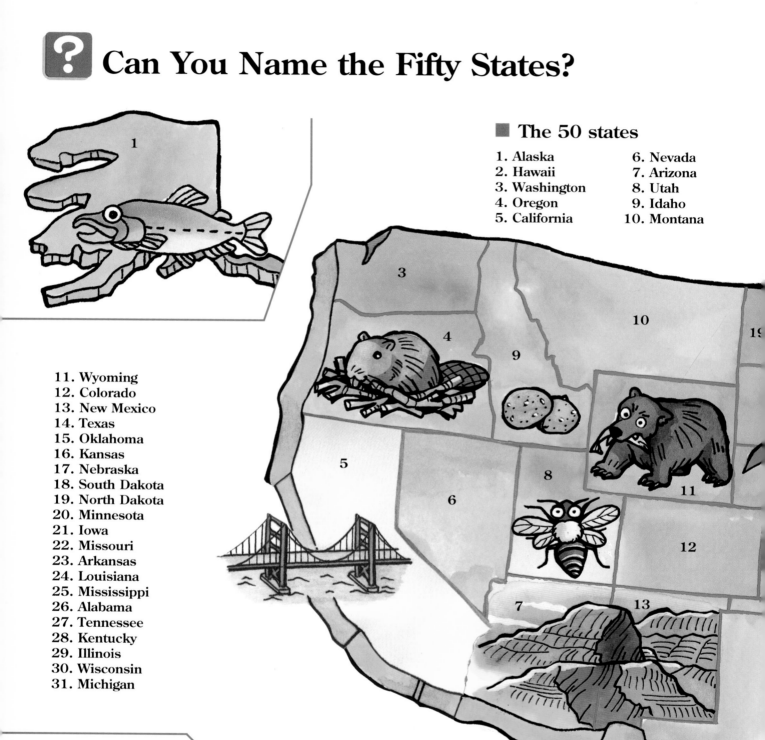

■ The 50 states

1. Alaska
2. Hawaii
3. Washington
4. Oregon
5. California

6. Nevada
7. Arizona
8. Utah
9. Idaho
10. Montana

11. Wyoming
12. Colorado
13. New Mexico
14. Texas
15. Oklahoma
16. Kansas
17. Nebraska
18. South Dakota
19. North Dakota
20. Minnesota
21. Iowa
22. Missouri
23. Arkansas
24. Louisiana
25. Mississippi
26. Alabama
27. Tennessee
28. Kentucky
29. Illinois
30. Wisconsin
31. Michigan

32. Indiana
33. Ohio
34. Pennsylvania
35. New York
36. Vermont
37. Maine
38. New Hampshire
39. Massachusetts
40. Rhode Island

41. Connecticut
42. New Jersey
43. Delaware
44. Maryland
45. West Virginia
46. Virginia

47. North Carolina
48. South Carolina
49. Georgia
50. Florida

ANSWER The United States is a union of 50 states. Each state has its own regional government and its own distinctive features. Many states are nicknamed for their specialties. Oregon, for example, is known as the Beaver State, Arizona as the Grand Canyon State, and Kansas as the Sunflower State.

■ Stars and stripes

▲ The 50 stars on the flag of the United States stand for the 50 states. The stripes symbolize the original 13 states.

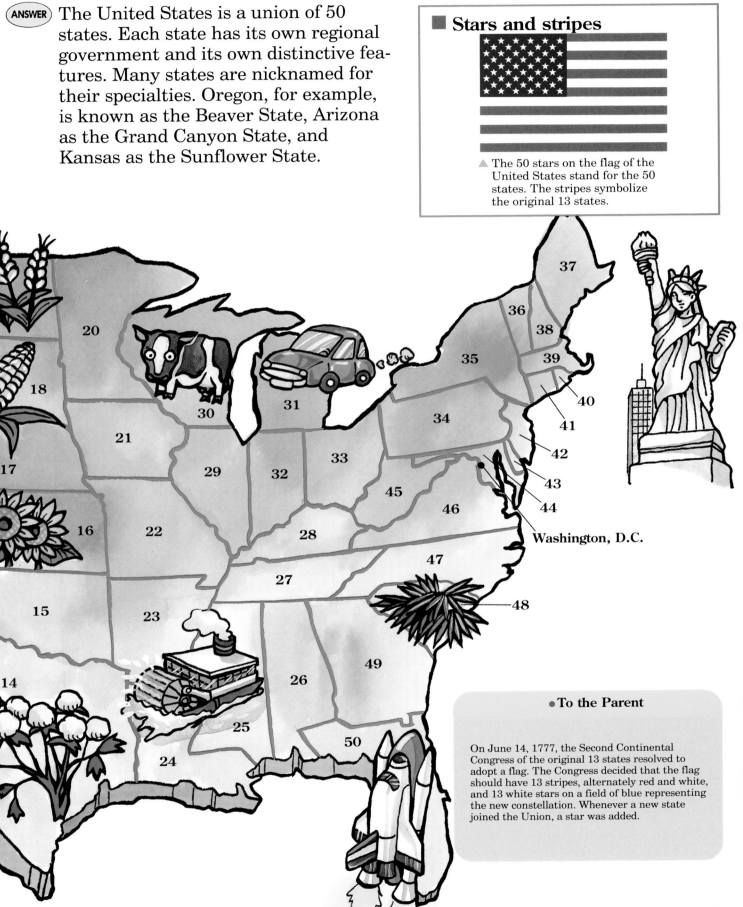

Washington, D.C.

● To the Parent

On June 14, 1777, the Second Continental Congress of the original 13 states resolved to adopt a flag. The Congress decided that the flag should have 13 stripes, alternately red and white, and 13 white stars on a field of blue representing the new constellation. Whenever a new state joined the Union, a star was added.

How Many People Live in the World?

ANSWER In 1993 the United Nations' count of the world's population passed a remarkable number: 5,555,555,555 people. That is more than 5 billion people. The illustration below shows how these people are spread across the globe. The area with the highest population is Asia.

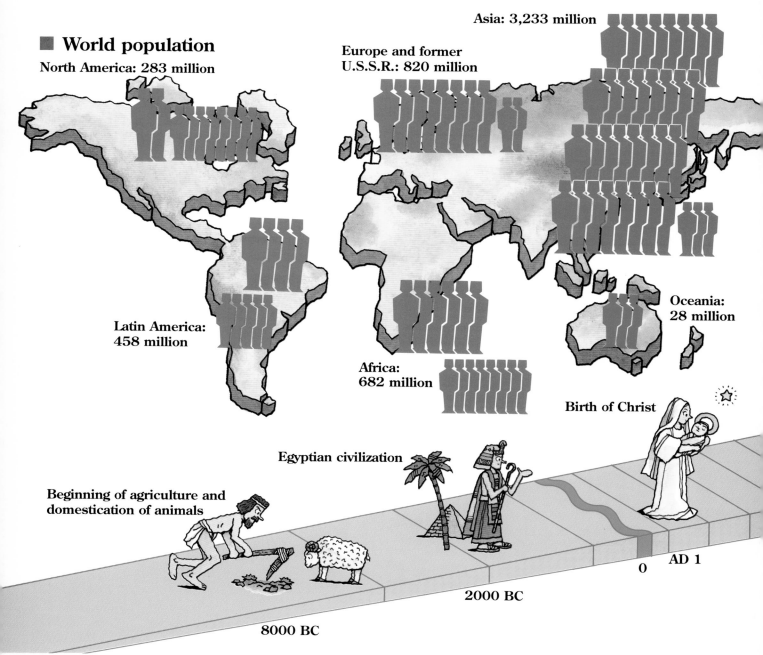

■ **World population**

North America: 283 million

Europe and former U.S.S.R.: 820 million

Asia: 3,233 million

Latin America: 458 million

Africa: 682 million

Oceania: 28 million

Birth of Christ

Egyptian civilization

Beginning of agriculture and domestication of animals

8000 BC

2000 BC

0

AD 1

■ A growing population

By the end of the 20th century, in the year 2000, world population will increase by the numbers shown below. The population of Asia and Africa is expected to expand rapidly, but in Europe, North America, and Oceania the population will grow more slowly.

North America	**12 million**
Latin America	**80 million**
Europe and former U.S.S.R.	**21.5 million**
Asia	**480 million**
Africa	**185 million**
Oceania	**2 million**

■ Sudden rise

About 2,000 years ago, at the time of the birth of Christ, only some 250 million people lived on earth. This figure did not double until about 1650. Wars, famines, and diseases kept populations low. Gradually, with better health care, improved cleanliness, and greater food supplies, populations increased. Forecasters expect the world's total population to top 6 billion by the 21st century.

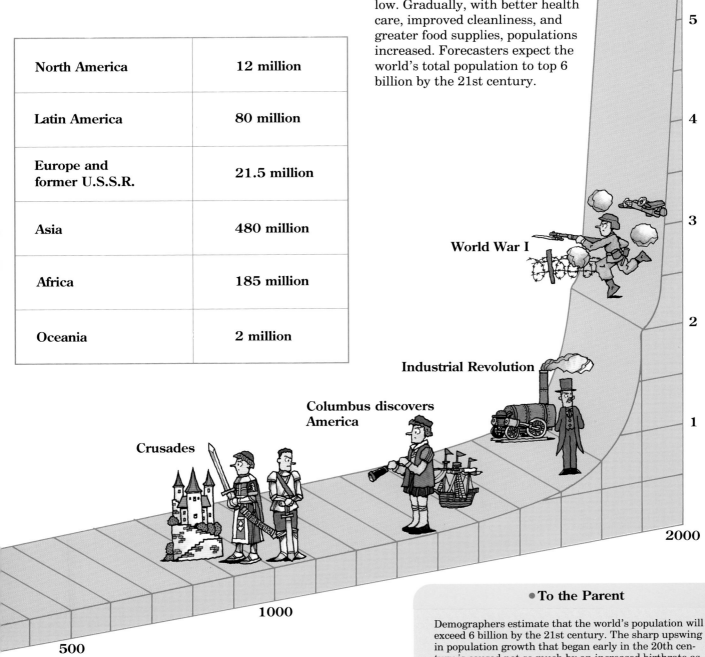

Billions

World War I

Industrial Revolution

Columbus discovers America

Crusades

500

1000

2000

● **To the Parent**

Demographers estimate that the world's population will exceed 6 billion by the 21st century. The sharp upswing in population growth that began early in the 20th century is caused not so much by an increased birthrate as by an extended life span, brought on by better medical care and a higher standard of living. The challenge now is to curb the rapid population increase. Population growth is low in developed countries but must be reduced in underdeveloped countries.

? Do Countries Own the Ocean?

ANSWER All countries bordering the ocean lay claim to some territory off the coast. According to the United Nations, such countries may own up to 12 nautical miles of so-called territorial waters off their shoreline. Distance at sea is measured by the nautical mile, which is 1.15 miles. But some countries make use of as many as 200 miles of territorial waters off their coasts.

Territorial limit

Territorial waters

■ Rights to the ocean

Countries bordered by the ocean control territorial waters, which are several miles of ocean belonging to them just as the land does. Ships from other countries cannot enter these waters without permission but are allowed passage for peaceful navigation.

■ Marking limits

Territorial limits, which define the size of territorial waters, cannot be marked by a fence or other visible boundaries. The limit is an imaginary line measured from land's end.

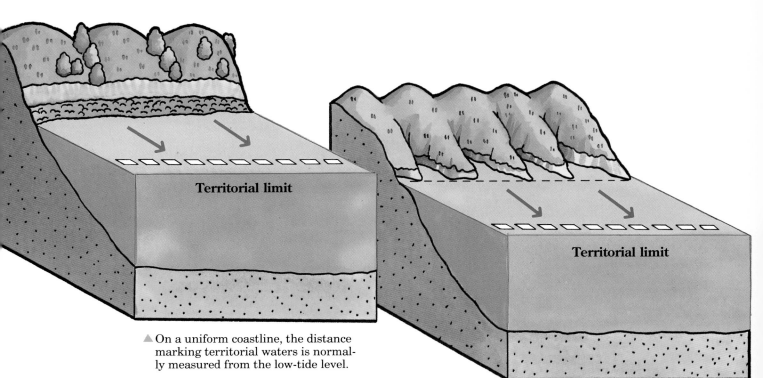

▲ On a uniform coastline, the distance marking territorial waters is normally measured from the low-tide level.

▲ On a deeply indented coastline, distance is measured from a uniform line beginning at the spit of land that reaches out farthest into the water.

■ The 200-mile limit

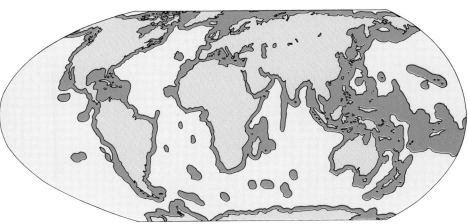

In addition to their territorial waters, many countries now claim parts of the ocean for fishing and mineral exploration. This area extends for 200 miles and is called an economic zone. Other countries cannot catch fish or drill for oil within 200 miles of the shoreline without permission.

● **To the Parent**

Territorial limits are not uniformly defined. Many nations have proclaimed 12 nautical miles as the limit of their territorial waters. Other countries want to push the limit to 200 miles for economic reasons, to help them secure not only fishing rights but also mineral rights. When one nation wants to exploit fishing or mineral rights in another country's economic zone, it must pay for the rights.

31

Are Oceans and Seas Different?

ANSWER People refer to the ocean and the sea as if they were the same. But geographers define seas as large bodies of water that are partly enclosed by land. More than 50 seas ring the continents. Seas are smaller and shallower than oceans and are usually more salty than the ocean. A few enclosed bodies of water are called seas, but they are lakes. Among them are the Caspian Sea, whose shores touch Russia and Iran, and the Aral Sea between Kazakhstan and Uzbekistan.

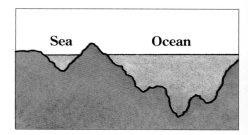

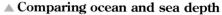

▲ Comparing ocean and sea depth

■ Ocean currents

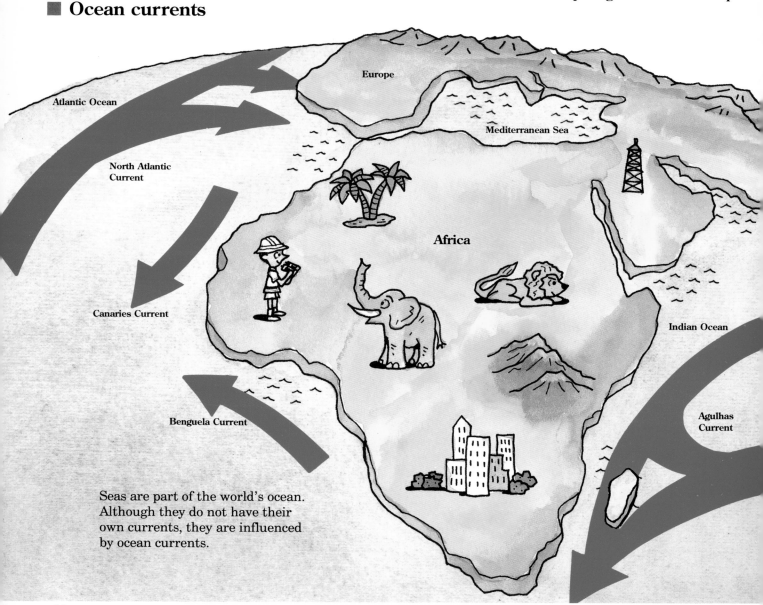

Seas are part of the world's ocean. Although they do not have their own currents, they are influenced by ocean currents.

32

World oceans and their seas

The seas cluster around the coasts of India and East Asia and the northern coasts of Europe and North America, with only a few along the coasts of Central America and Antarctica. Some seas cut far into the land; others are linked to the ocean by narrow passages between islands; the rest have wide openings to the ocean.

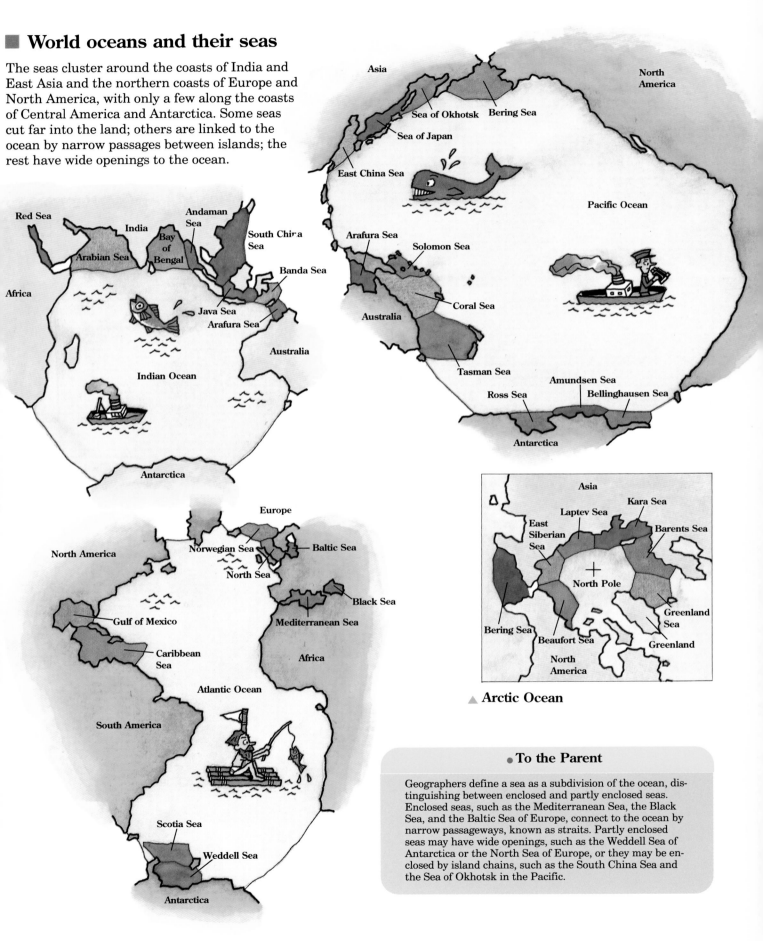

▲ Arctic Ocean

33

How Much of the Earth Is Covered with Forest?

ANSWER Forests cover about one-third of the earth's land surface. The world's forests are an important resource. They influence climate, preserve the soil, and provide the planet with oxygen. But forests are shrinking fast. Stands that have taken hundreds of years to grow are being destroyed.

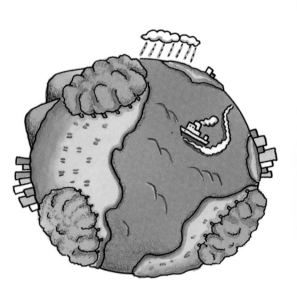

■ The world's forests

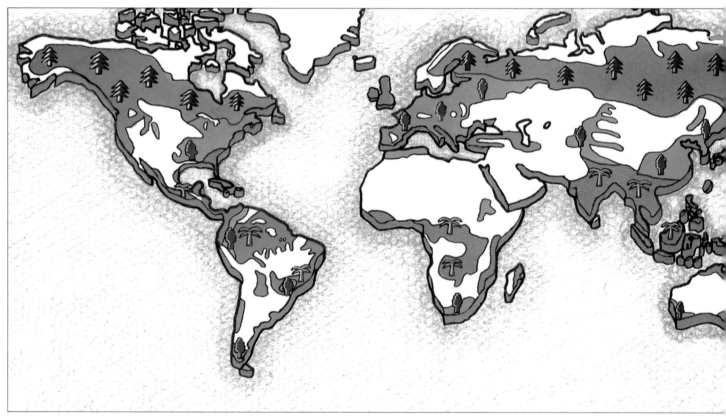

▲ Forests grow on every continent except Antarctica, where it is too cold and dry. Trees need at least 30 inches of rain per year to grow, although certain pines can survive on less. Tropical rain forests grow near the equator, where there is plenty of rainfall and it is warm year-round. Evergreen forests grow at high elevations and in a band across the northernmost regions in cold climates. A mixture of evergreens and deciduous trees—that is, trees which lose their leaves in winter—grows in regions with four seasons. Above a certain elevation forests will not grow. Once a forest has been cut down and the land has turned to desert, it is almost impossible to restore it to its earlier green state.

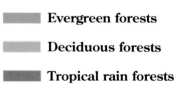

Evergreen forests

Deciduous forests

Tropical rain forests

34

Types of forests

Forests differ in type depending on the climate
and the surface features of the regions where
they grow. Half of the world's forests grow
in hot places; another third grow where it is
usually cold; the rest grow in regions where the
seasons change.

▲ **Rain forest**

◄ **Evergreen forest**

◄ **Deciduous forest**

● **To the Parent**

Several thousand years ago forests were twice as extensive
as they are today. For most of human history, people have
cut down trees for firewood and to build houses. But in the
past several hundred years people have been depleting
forests at an alarming rate to clear land for settlement and
grazing land and to obtain lumber and firewood. Acid rain
and other pollution add to the rapid demise of forests.

35

Are There Deserts in All Parts of the World?

ANSWER Deserts are found on every continent and cover almost one-third of the earth's land surface. Rocky or sandy, these dry regions form not only in hot-weather countries but also in cold lands. Although deserts are a harsh environment, many people live in desert regions.

▲ It seldom rains in a desert, in some regions no more than once every 10 years. Trees can grow only where underground springs flow, in areas called oases.

■ Desert near the coast

Even regions near the coast can be desert, like the Atacama Desert in Chile. This desert is caused by a cold ocean current that flows past the coast of Peru and Chile. The winds blowing onto the land are cool and dry, preventing any rainfall.

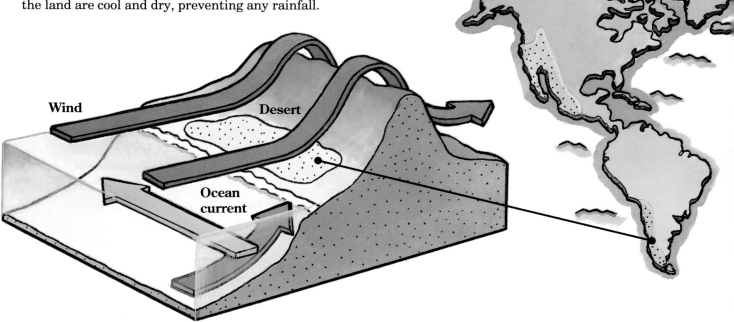

Wind

Desert

Ocean current

■ Desert near the equator

It often rains in countries along the equator, but the rain is followed by cool, dry winds, which move the air away from the equator. This air keeps clouds from forming, so that it seldom rains in areas just beyond the equator, such as the Sahara.

Wind

Desert

■ Interior desert

Some areas in the interior of a continent are so far away from any ocean that moisture-laden air cannot reach them. As a result the region gets almost no rain and becomes a desert. One example is the Gobi Desert in Central Asia.

Wind

Desert

● **To the Parent**

Deserts are divided into subtropical, coastal, rain shadow, interior, and polar deserts. The most extensive deserts lie between latitudes 15° and 30° north or south of the equator and include the Sahara and the Kalahari of Africa, the Rub'al-Khali of Saudi Arabia, and the deserts of Australia's Western Plateau. Although the continent of Antarctica is largely covered by polar ice, it is classified as a desert, because it receives less than an inch of rainfall annually.

How Are Sand Dunes Formed?

ANSWER Sand dunes are hills of sand. They form on beaches and in deserts from the buildup of sand carried by the wind. Since the wind shapes the dunes, they take on different forms depending on the wind's speed and direction.

▲ The pattern on a stretch of sandy beach shows the direction and force of the wind. Dunes take shape when the wind picks up sand in one place and drops it in another, forming ridges and peaks.

■ **Sand dunes**

Grains of sand carried along by the wind roll down the rear slope of a dune. As the grains of sand shift, they give the dune a wavy pattern.

Once a dune has formed, it may move. The sand blows up one side of the dune and down the other side, causing the dune to drift forward slowly.

■ Shapes of dunes

The wavelike patterns that form on sand dunes are determined by the direction and strength of the wind, the amount of sand, and the size of the grains.

▼Crescent-shaped dunes form on level plains where the wind blows steadily. These dunes can reach 100 feet high.

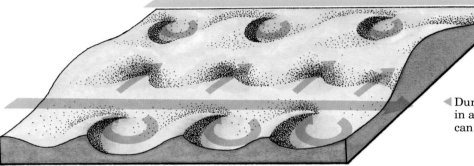

◀Dunes patterned like a saw blade form in areas with a lot of sand. The peaks can reach heights up to 300 feet.

■ Coastal dunes

Where dunes form on sandy beaches, they act as a barrier to protect the shore from battering ocean waves.

●To the Parent

Sand dunes begin to form around a slight obstacle, such as a twig or a pebble. A dune starts to take shape when wind blows across the obstacle that interrupts the airflow and drops sand behind it. In this so-called wind shadow, grains of sand collect and attract more grains, building mounds that join together to form a dune. The wind constantly arranges and rearranges the shapes and patterns of the dunes, moving some as much as 80 feet in a year.

What Is the Rainy Season?

ANSWER
In some Asian countries the weather changes little: It never gets cold, but it may be cool and dry, hot and dry, or hot and wet. During the hot and wet season, it rains almost constantly. The rain is caused by the summer heat, which makes moist air rise from the ocean. This moisture is blown over the land and falls as rain.

▲ During the rainy season in India, so much rain comes down at one time that the streets become flooded in many places.

■ The rainy season

During the rainy season, the cool ocean is heated by the hot summer sun, and the water evaporates. This process creates moisture in the air, which is blown toward the warmer land. There, the moisture drops as rain.

▲ During the dry season, it almost never rains in India, and the streets are dry and dusty.

●**To the Parent**

In summer some Asian countries get so hot that the air rising from the land creates a large area of low pressure. The low pressure brings in cool, moist wind from the ocean. The moisture rises on the warm upward air currents over land and then condenses into heavy rains that last an entire season. Areas affected include Southeast Asia, northern India, southern China, Japan, and the southern tip of Korea.

■ The dry season

Winds blow from high-pressure to low-pressure areas. In winter the land is cool and pressure is high, so the wind blows from the land to the ocean. These winter winds do not carry rain.

41

? Do Hurricanes Rage Everywhere?

ANSWER Hurricanes occur when moist air heated over the ocean rises and is replaced by cooler air spiraling into its place. As the air whirls, it creates low pressure. The low pressure allows the spiraling wind to increase and build into a tropical storm. Once hurricanes are born, they are carried along by the flow of the surrounding air, causing severe damage as they sweep onto the land. Hurricanes form over the Caribbean and along the Pacific and the Atlantic coasts of North America.

▲Hurricanes begin in warm tropical seas; they need a water temperature of 80° F. or more before they can build up.

■ Path of a hurricane

1 A hurricane in the Caribbean develops in summer or fall above warm seas. Moist air from the sea forms clouds, which turn into low-pressure whirlpools.

2 The hurricane is pushed along by strong winds, gathering more speed and energy along the way. As the storm nears the Gulf of Mexico, winds from the east prevent it from swerving and keep it on course toward the United States.

3 As the storm nears the land, it meets winds blowing from the west. The western winds blow it back toward the east, and the storm moves in a large arc toward Florida.

4 After crossing Florida, the storm loses strength. By the time it moves back out to sea, it is much weaker and in time dies out over cooler waters.

■ The world's storms

Whirling storms, called hurricanes in the United States, rage in many parts of the world. In Asia these storms are called typhoons, in India cyclones, and in Australia willy-willies. The illustration below shows where they occur.

● **To the Parent**

The World Meteorological Organization rates winds of 75 miles per hour over tropical waters as hurricanes or typhoons. Since these storms do not usually form unless the water temperature is 80° F. or warmer, they begin only above tropical seas between 5° and 25° north and south of the equator. They do not form at the equator because wind conditions there are not right.

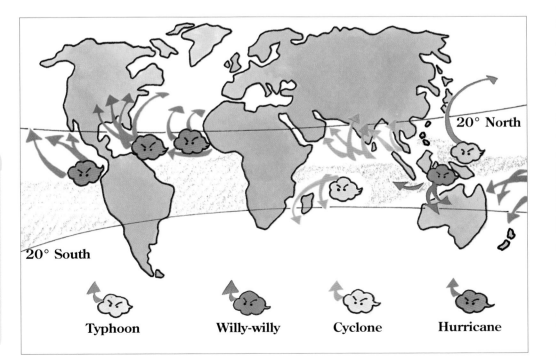

20° North

20° South

Typhoon   Willy-willy   Cyclone   Hurricane

Does All Rice Grow the Same Way?

ANSWER Rice is the most important food for half of the world's population. This valuable grain will grow wherever it is warm and moist. Depending on the climate and the amount of water available, rice may react in different ways. Of the more than 14,000 varieties of rice, some ripen in about 100 days, and others take twice as long.

▲ Ripening rice

■ One and two crops a year

	April	May	June	July	August	September
	Plant seedlings	Transplant				Drain fields

	March	April	May	June	July	August	September
	Plant seedlings	Transplant		Drain fields	Harvest	Transplant	

Double crops

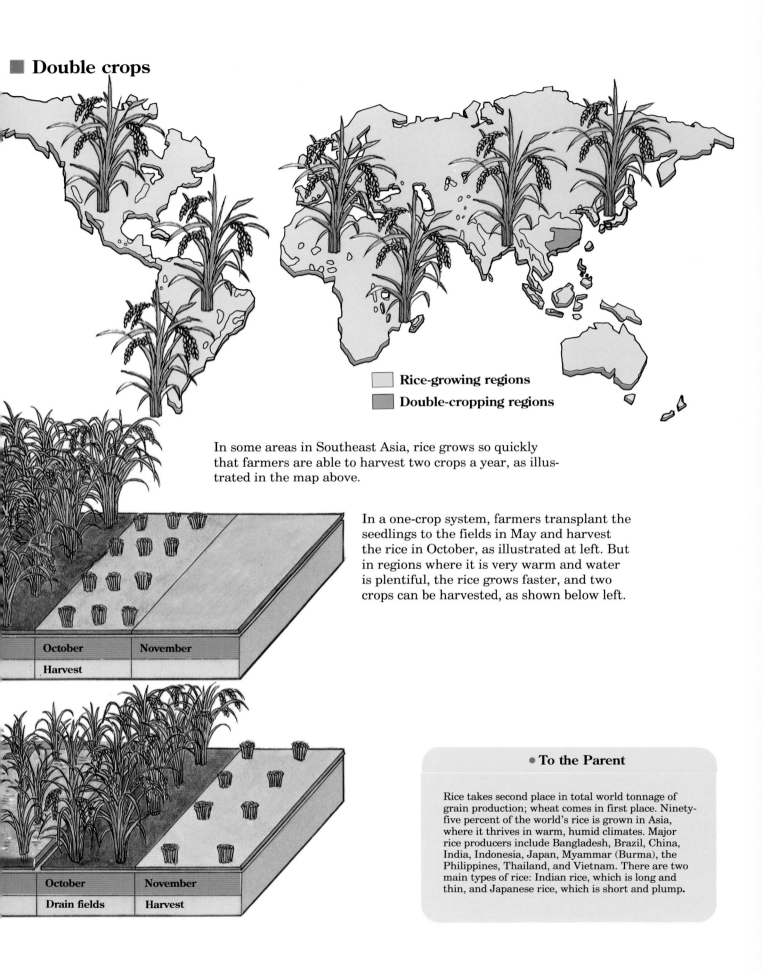

Rice-growing regions

Double-cropping regions

In some areas in Southeast Asia, rice grows so quickly that farmers are able to harvest two crops a year, as illustrated in the map above.

In a one-crop system, farmers transplant the seedlings to the fields in May and harvest the rice in October, as illustrated at left. But in regions where it is very warm and water is plentiful, the rice grows faster, and two crops can be harvested, as shown below left.

October	November
Harvest	

October	November
Drain fields	Harvest

● **To the Parent**

Rice takes second place in total world tonnage of grain production; wheat comes in first place. Ninety-five percent of the world's rice is grown in Asia, where it thrives in warm, humid climates. Major rice producers include Bangladesh, Brazil, China, India, Indonesia, Japan, Myammar (Burma), the Philippines, Thailand, and Vietnam. There are two main types of rice: Indian rice, which is long and thin, and Japanese rice, which is short and plump.

Is Wheat Cultivated in All Countries?

ANSWER Wheat is the most important grain crop in the world, providing three-quarters of people's basic nutrition. The grain is ground into flour to be used in breads, pastries, cereals, noodles, and many other foods. Wheat can withstand cold weather and does not need as much water to thrive as rice does. It grows in almost all parts of the world.

▲Harvesting wheat

■ Wheat-growing regions

The main wheat-growing regions are shown on this map in yellow. The red line divides cultivation into spring- and winter-wheat regions. Wheat grows on all continents except Antarctica and the areas above and below the blue lines.

Wheat belts

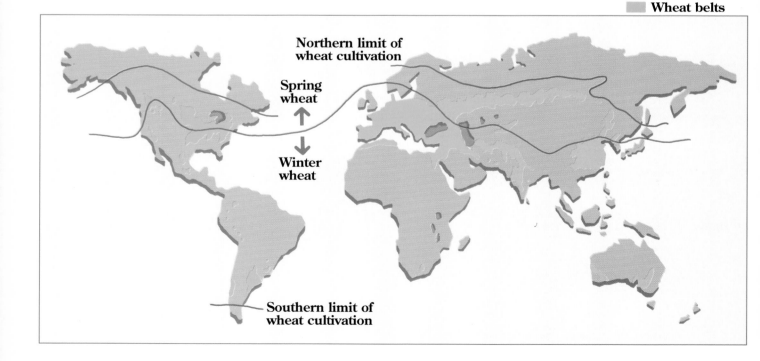

Northern limit of wheat cultivation

Spring wheat ↑

Winter wheat ↓

Southern limit of wheat cultivation

Top wheat producers

China	▢ ▢ ▢ ▢ ▢ ▢ ▢	3,530 million bushels
Former Soviet Union	▢ ▢ ▢ ▢ ▢	2,840 million
United States	▢ ▢ ▢ ▢ ▢	2,600 million
India	▢ ▢ ▢ ▢	2,020 million
France	▢ ▢	1,160 million
Canada	▢ ▢	1,030 million
Turkey	▢	600 million
Australia	▢	590 million
Pakistan	▢	570 million
Germany	▢	550 million

Wheat can be grown almost anywhere, and at any time of the year it is being harvested somewhere in the world. The chart above shows the major wheat-producing nations. Most of the world's wheat crop is winter wheat, which is sown in the fall because it needs cool winter temperatures to germinate. Winter wheat is harvested early in the summer. Spring wheat is sown in the spring and harvested in the late summer.

■ Types of wheat

There are more than 30,000 varieties of wheat. The two major species are durum wheat for noodles and bread wheat for breads and pastries.

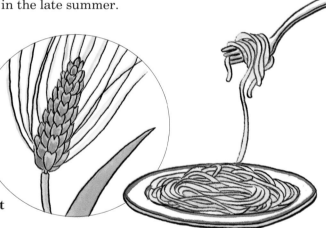

▶ **Durum wheat**

▲ **Bread wheat**

● **To the Parent**

Grain is the main source of food for every civilization. Because wheat can be cultivated under various difficult conditions, it has been grown since the earliest days of farming. Following wheat and rice in importance, corn is the third major grain and is the staple food of people in Central and South America. Oats, rye, sorghum, millet, and barley also play a role in serving basic food needs and are used as cereals, in breads, and to feed livestock.

What Do Farmers Do When It Doesn't Rain Enough?

ANSWER Farmers need water for everything they grow. In areas with little rainfall, farmers have found ways around the problem. In one method, called dryland farming, farmers seed only half their land with crops, while the other half is allowed to rest and soak up what little rain there is. In another method, they water their crops by artificial means, channeling water from places that have a lot to the fields that need it.

■ Dryland farming

To allow rainwater to collect in the soil, half of the land is left unplanted for two or three years.

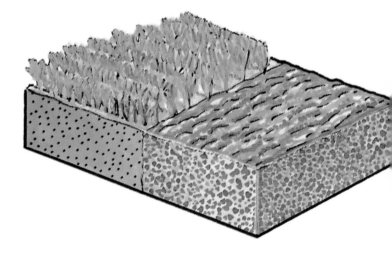

■ Irrigated farming

▼ A pipeline carries water to the fields from a dam constructed in the mountains to store rainwater. For some fields the water must be pumped over long distances.

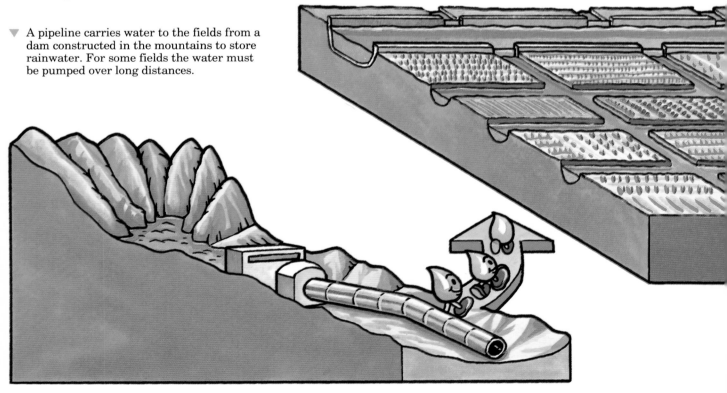

► Center-pivot sprinklers draw underground water to the surface and spray the fields. The sprinklers move in a circle, and the crops grow where the water falls, making the fields look round. This and other types of sprinkler systems are used in much of the arid West of the United States to keep crops watered.

▲ A *kanat,* sometimes spelled *qanat,* taps ground water from a mountain and channels it to fields. This ancient type of irrigation is used in North Africa and western and central Asia.

● **To the Parent**

Farming methods in arid regions are divided between dryland and irrigated farming. Both methods have been practiced since the beginning of agriculture. Early irrigation systems involved flooding entire fields or drawing water from canals and channeling it between rows. Dryland farming calls for alternating between fallow and productive fields. Modern sprinkler systems turn near-desert land into fertile farmland.

49

❓ What Are the Staple Foods of People around the World?

ANSWER A staple food is the food that the people of a country eat regularly and in large amounts. Usually the staple food grows in that country and is well suited to the climate and the soil.

■ Staples of the world

▲ Caribou meat

▲ Corn tortillas

◀ The staple foods of Eskimos in the Arctic region are whale and caribou meat. In Mexico, people eat corn as a vegetable and as cornmeal in tortillas.

▲ **Bread**　　　　　　　▲ **Noodles**　　　　　▲ **Rice**

In the United States and Europe *(above left)*, the staple food is wheat, which is milled into flour for bread. In northern China *(center)*, wheat is made into noodles. In Japan *(right)* and other Asian countries, rice is a staple.

▼ People in western Africa enjoy yams, which are a major food source.

▲ **Dates**　　　　　　　▲ In Arab countries, people eat the fruit of the date palm as one of their staple foods.

▲ **Yams**

●**To the Parent**

A staple food is usually a grain or a vegetable that is native to a region. Sometimes one staple food replaces another as changes in land or climate occur. The staple foods of the Eskimos are one example. Whale and caribou meat were once the mainstays of their diet, but with the introduction of Western dietary habits they now eat all the other foods Americans eat.

Why Does Australia Have So Many Sheep?

ANSWER Australia's dry, poor soil is not suitable for farming. But Australian grasslands support the world's largest number of sheep.

■ **Australia's sheep**

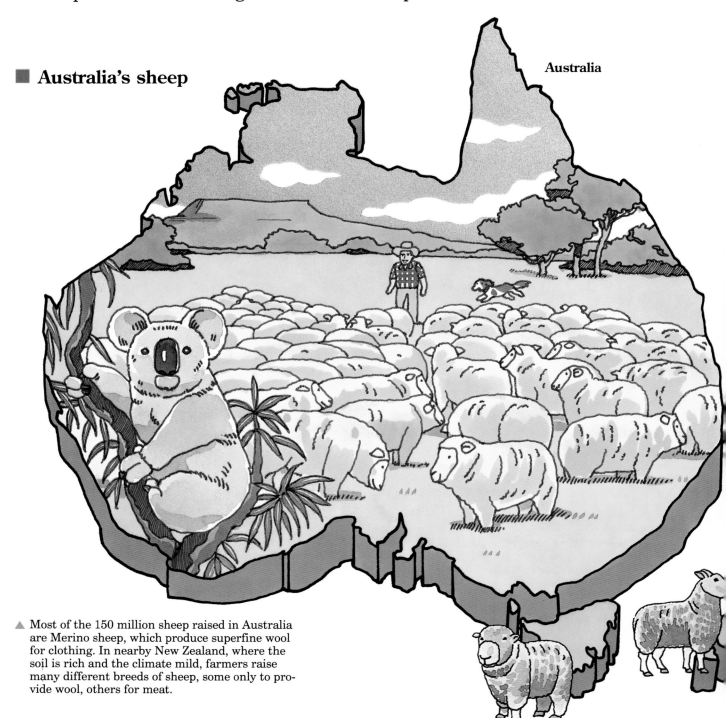

Australia

▲ Most of the 150 million sheep raised in Australia are Merino sheep, which produce superfine wool for clothing. In nearby New Zealand, where the soil is rich and the climate mild, farmers raise many different breeds of sheep, some only to provide wool, others for meat.

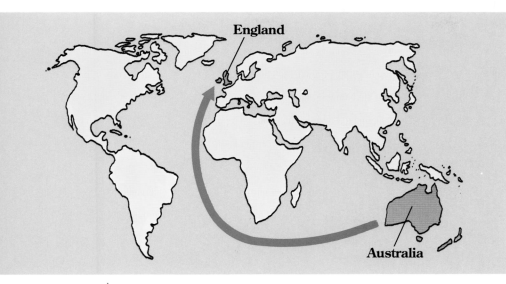

England

Australia

■ A bit of history

Portuguese and Dutch explorers first visited Australia in the 16th and 17th centuries. Captain James Cook claimed the continent for Great Britain in 1770, and it became a colony. Many people emigrated from England to start a new life in Australia.

▶ To ship products from Australia to England meant a long sea voyage. Australians realized it would be smart to produce something that was lightweight and would not spoil on the way. When they thought of sheep's wool, they had the answer. Sheep's wool weighs little and keeps well.

New Zealand

▶ In the early spring, sheep-shearers cut the sheep's wool. The wool shorn from a single sheep is often cut in one large piece and called a fleece. A Merino sheep's fleece may weigh as much as 30 pounds. The first shearing of a young sheep produces the finest wool, which is known as lamb's wool.

● To the Parent

When Captain James Cook explored Australia in 1770, he claimed it for Great Britain. The British government designated the new land a penal colony, and Australia was obligated to contribute exports to Britain. Wool turned out to be the most profitable choice.

? Where in France Do Grapes Grow Well?

ANSWER The south of France has long, sunny summers and mild, wet winters, which is the ideal climate for growing grapes. Grapevines flourish all around the Mediterranean Sea because they can adapt to long spells of drought, then store water later on when rain is plentiful.

▲ Grape harvest

■ Mediterranean vineyards

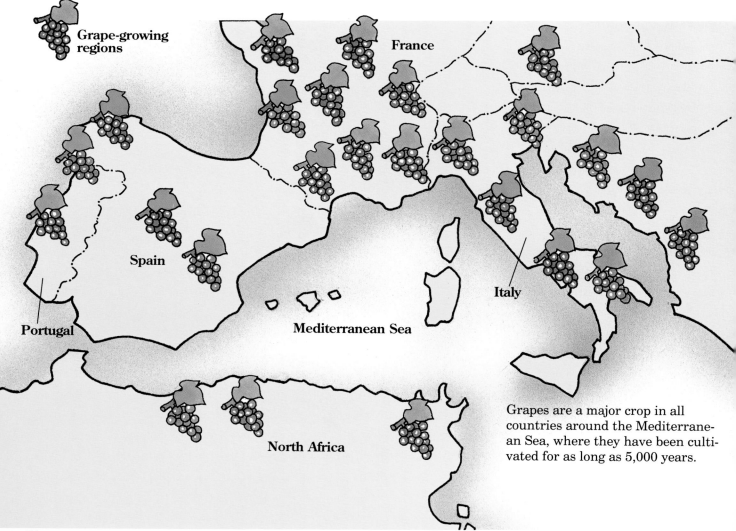

Grape-growing regions

France

Spain

Portugal

Italy

Mediterranean Sea

North Africa

Grapes are a major crop in all countries around the Mediterranean Sea, where they have been cultivated for as long as 5,000 years.

■ Climate for growth

The climate around the Mediterranean Sea is governed by high-pressure warm winds blowing from the northeast in summer—which keep the soil warm and dry—and low-pressure winds from the west in winter—which bring a lot of rain.

Winter

In winter, west winds blow, bringing much-needed rain. Grapevines store food and water during this period.

Summer

The Mediterranean summer is warm and dry, helping grapevines to grow. The grapes are picked in the fall.

▲ Grapevines can grow easily in regions where there is little rain in summer. The vine's roots can grow up to 100 feet into the ground and will dig until they find a wet layer. Then they send out many small roots to soak up the available water.

What Is the Midnight Sun?

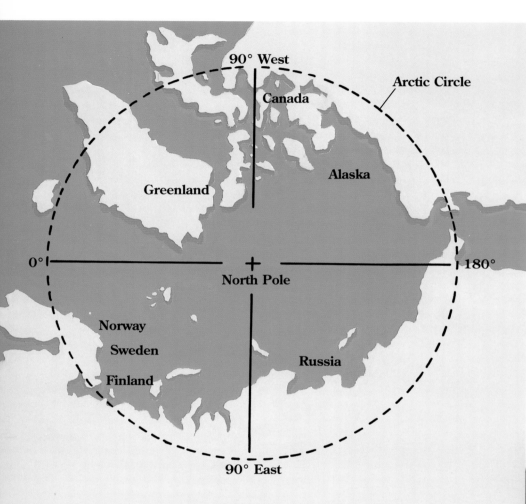

■ The Arctic

The Arctic *(left)* includes the Arctic Ocean, Alaska, Canada, Greenland, Russia, and north Scandinavia. At the summer solstice, on June 21, the sun never sets. At the winter solstice, on December 21, the sun never rises.

ANSWER Countries near the North Pole have long days of light in summer and long days of darkness in winter. At the summer solstice, the sun shines for 24 hours. Its pale light at midnight is called the midnight sun. At the winter solstice, the sun never rises, and it is dark all day.

■ The Antarctic

At the South Pole *(below)* the seasons are opposite from those of the North Pole. The sun stays above the horizon when it is summer at the South Pole, but winter at the North Pole.

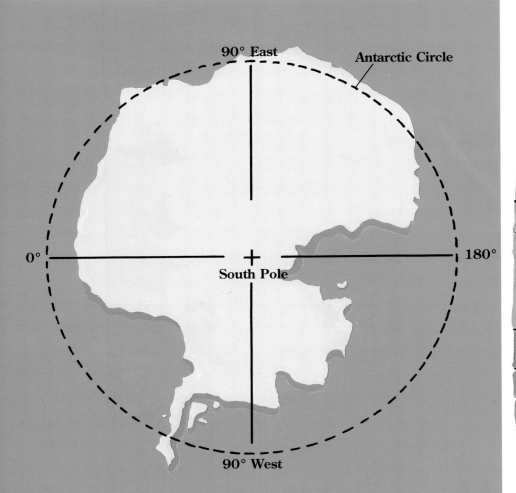

Because of the earth's tilt toward the sun, the area within the Arctic Circle stays exposed for long hours to the sun during the summer, while the area within the Antarctic Circle stays dark.

● **To the Parent**

The earth is tilted on its axis by 23.5° as it orbits the sun. This position exposes the Arctic Circle to the full light of the sun during the summer solstice and drops it into complete darkness during the winter solstice. The opposite is true for the Antarctic Circle, where the winter solstice occurs when it is summer at the North Pole.

Which Lake Is the Largest in the World?

Great Britain

Caspian Sea

ANSWER The world's largest lake is an inland salt lake known as the Caspian Sea, bordered by Azerbaijan, Iran, Kazakhstan, Russia, and Turkmenistan. More than 11 million years ago the Caspian Sea was connected to the Black Sea, which is linked to the Mediterranean Sea. A continental shift caused the Caspian Sea to be cut off. Since then it has existed as an inland sea.

■ Bigger than Great Britain

The Caspian Sea is so enormous that all of the British Isles could fit inside it, with room to spare.

▲ The port city of Baku on the Caspian Sea

▲ Duluth on the shores of Lake Superior

▲ Lake Victoria in the African plain

■ The 10 largest lakes

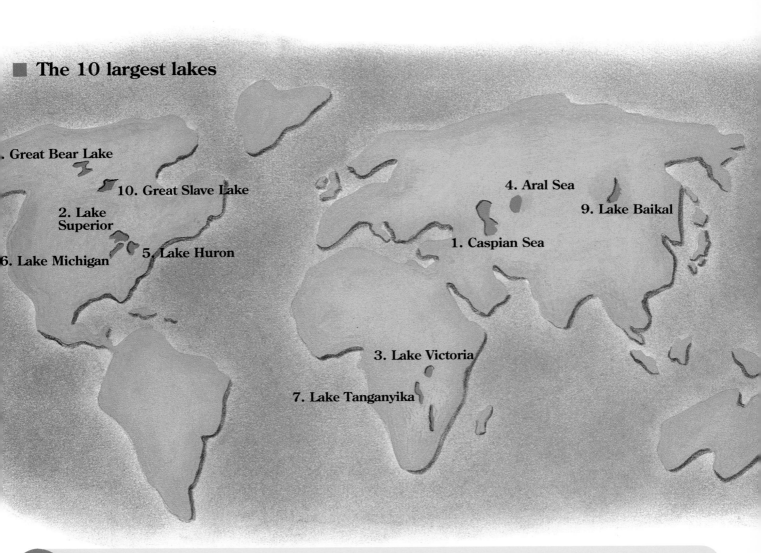

. Great Bear Lake

10. Great Slave Lake

2. Lake Superior

6. Lake Michigan

5. Lake Huron

4. Aral Sea

9. Lake Baikal

1. Caspian Sea

3. Lake Victoria

7. Lake Tanganyika

Which One Is the Deepest?

The deepest lake in the world is Lake Baikal in Russian Siberia. The lake reaches 5,315 feet at its deepest point. Every winter it is frozen solid from January through April. Lake Baikal is famous for its unusually clear water, and it is home to unique shrimp and other crustaceans that filter impurities from the water.

● To the Parent

The world's largest lake, the Caspian Sea, is 750 miles long and between 130 and 300 miles wide, with a depth of 3,200 feet. The second largest is Lake Superior, between the United States and Canada; and the third largest is Lake Victoria in Africa, bordered by Kenya, Tanzania, and Uganda. The Aral Sea in the former Soviet Union is counted as the fourth largest, although it has shrunk by about 60 percent through evaporation and irrigation.

▲ The snowy banks of Lake Baikal

❓ Which River Is the Longest?

ANSWER The world's longest river is the Nile, which flows for 4,160 miles from south to north halfway across the continent of Africa. Beginning in the tiny nation of Burundi, the Nile flows through nine countries, many of them near-deserts, and ends in Egypt. The river brings life-giving water to the parched lands along its shores.

■ The Nile River

Sahara

Nile River

Lake Victoria

Madagascar

The world's longest rivers

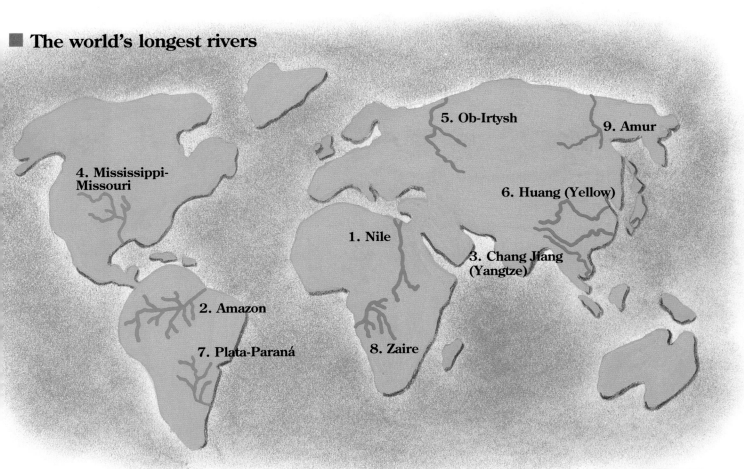

5. Ob-Irtysh

9. Amur

4. Mississippi-Missouri

6. Huang (Yellow)

1. Nile

3. Chang Jiang (Yangtze)

2. Amazon

7. Plata-Paraná

8. Zaire

 ## Which River Is the Biggest?

▲The Amazon

The Amazon is the world's largest river in both the volume of water it carries and the size of its drainage basin. A river's drainage basin is the area through which flow the river and the streams that join it, called tributaries. The Amazon has many tributaries, which wind through the farthest reaches of the South American tropical rain forest.

●To the Parent

The longest rivers in small countries are tiny in comparison with the giants shown here. The longest river in Japan, for example, is the Shinano. It is only 228 miles long, a bit more than one-fifth of the length of the Nile. Japan is a small island country, and its rivers are narrow and swift. As a rule, swift rivers run a relatively straight course, and only slow-moving rivers meander lazily through vast territory.

Which Mountain Is the Tallest?

▲ Everest

ANSWER Mountains rise on every continent and also from the ocean floor. The world's highest mountain is Mount Everest, towering five and a half miles above sea level. Mount Everest straddles the countries of Nepal and Tibet in the Himalaya mountain range.

Mount Everest's peak is always covered with snow and ice, as are the tops of other mountain giants. The three highest mountains in the world are located in Asia: No. 1 is Mount Everest, No. 2 is K2 in Pakistan, and No. 3 is Kanchenjunga between India and Nepal.

■ The Himalayas

The Himalayas are often called the roof of the world because more than 40 peaks rise above 25,000 feet. The nearest of these to Mount Everest are shown below.

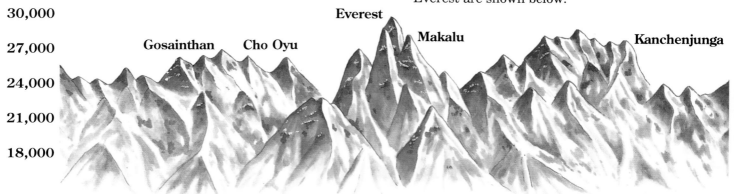

(Feet)

30,000

27,000

24,000

21,000

18,000

Gosainthan   Cho Oyu   Everest   Makalu   Kanchenjunga

■ World peaks

The highest mountain on each continent is: Asia, Mount Everest (1), 29,028 feet; South America, Mount Aconcagua (2), 22,834 feet; North America, Mount McKinley (4), 20,321 feet; Africa, Mount Kilimanjaro (5), 19,340 feet; Europe, Mont Blanc (3), 15,770 feet; Australia, Mount Kosciusko (6), 7,309 feet; and Antarctica, Vinson Massif *(not shown)*, 16,066 feet.

▲ Aconcagua

▲ Kanchenjunga

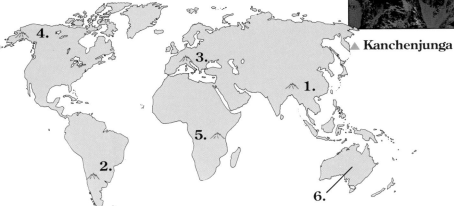

▲ McKinley

▲ Makalu

● To the Parent

Mont Blanc, rising to 15,770 feet, is usually listed as the highest peak in Europe, but another mountain may qualify as Europe's highest. Mount Elbrus soars to 18,510 feet in the Caucasus range just inside Russia's border with Georgia. Some authorities consider the region part of Europe; others say it is in Asia.

? Which Country Is the Highest?

ANSWER The tiny kingdom of Bhutan is perched so high in the mountains of the Himalayas that it is considered the highest country on earth. Not far away, in the same mountain range, the country of Nepal is almost as high. Nepal has only a slightly smaller percentage of land at the highest elevations and more at lower elevations.

■ **Top of the world**

◀ Nepal's capital, Kathmandu, lies in a valley in the Himalayas at an elevation of 4,500 feet. The city is surrounded by four of the six highest mountains on earth.

◀ Almost all the land in Bhutan, which lies between India and Tibet, is more than 6,500 feet above sea level. The highest peak is Mount Gangri, which rises to 24,740 feet.

Which is the lowest?

The Netherlands—its name means "low lands"—is very flat and some parts are as much as 22 feet below sea level. About half of the country would be flooded by the sea if the land were not protected by dikes. Almost all the world's land is above sea level. A few places on earth, but not entire countries, lie lower than the Netherlands. The Dead Sea between Israel and Jordan is more than 1,300 feet below sea level.

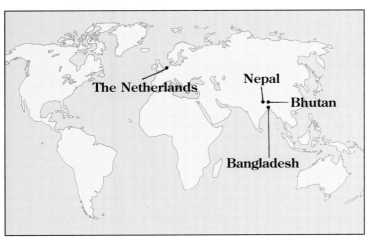

▲ The Netherlands' capital, Amsterdam, is crisscrossed by more than 150 canals, which fan out into shipping lanes.

▼ Khulna in Bangladesh lies at sea level in a river delta. The city is protected by embankments and built on mounds to escape seasonal flooding.

Hundreds of miles of dikes protect the low-lying Netherlands from flooding (right). In Bhutan and Nepal (top, far left) people live in places as high as 17,500 feet. No one lives higher than that. It is too cold to grow crops and people cannot breathe because the air has little oxygen.

How Can There Be a Tunnel under the Sea?

ANSWER Digging a tunnel under the sea requires deep drilling and heavy reinforcement of the shaft to shore up the tunnel's walls. Many short undersea tunnels are built across bays or below narrow ocean straits. Eurotunnel, a new passage under the English Channel, stretches for 31 miles across the Strait of Dover between Folkestone, England, and Calais, France.

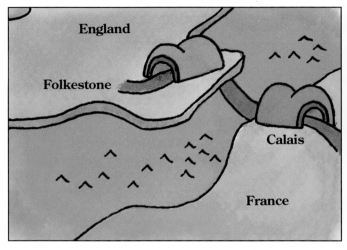

▲ The Eurotunnel

■ The Eurotunnel

The new Eurotunnel between England and France officially opened in 1994. Workers began digging from each coast and met in the middle to build a twin-track train tunnel. Passengers and cars are transported through the tunnel on shuttle trains. Travel time between London and Paris by train is about three hours, compared with six hours by ferry.

■ Strengthening a tunnel

When digging an undersea tunnel, workers must strengthen the walls so they will not collapse under the pressure of the sea's weight. As the tunnel is dug, the walls are quickly sprayed with concrete to fortify them and are supported with steel ribs. The walls are then reinforced with precast concrete segments to complete the tunnel.

■ Excavating machinery

The giant boring machine shown below drilled through the hard rock and soft ground beneath the ocean to cut passageways for the tunnel.

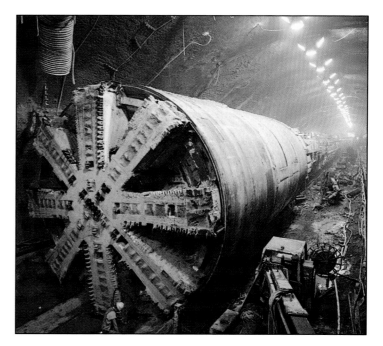

◀ Spraying with concrete

●**To the Parent**

One person who suggested a tunnel under the Channel about 200 years ago was Napoleon. But technical and political problems defeated the plan. Many other people since have proposed a tunnel with varying success, depending on the state of English and French relations at the time.

Did Africa and South America Once Touch Each Other?

ANSWER Today the earth's seven continents are separated, but ages ago they were all joined together. Forces underneath the earth's crust split the landmass into several pieces and caused the pieces to float apart, as shown in the illustrations below and at right.

▲ The earth's crust is broken into several pieces called plates. The plates sit on the earth's mantle, the part of the interior that is partly molten rock. Although the crust is about 40 miles thick, the mantle causes the plates to float, moving the continents.

■ Movement of continents

1

About 250 million years ago most of the land on earth was contained in a single large continent, which today is called Pangaea, meaning "all lands," and one great ocean called Panthalassa, or "all seas."

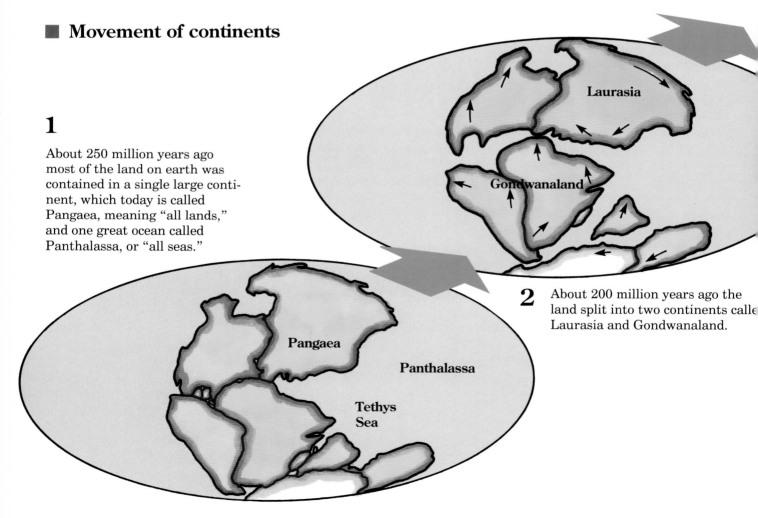

2 About 200 million years ago the land split into two continents calle Laurasia and Gondwanaland.

Laurasia

Gondwanaland

Pangaea

Panthalassa

Tethys Sea

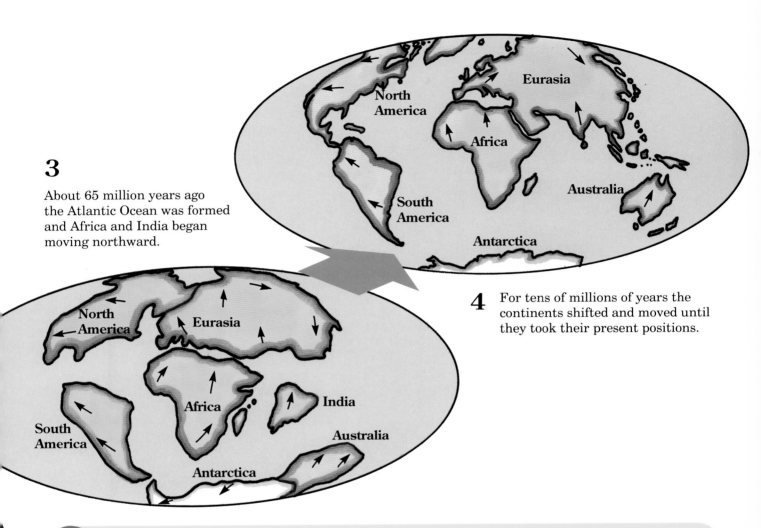

3

About 65 million years ago the Atlantic Ocean was formed and Africa and India began moving northward.

4 For tens of millions of years the continents shifted and moved until they took their present positions.

Will they move again?

Today the continents continue to shift. Scientists predict that in 50 million years, along with other changes, Australia will be nearer the equator. Crete may have pushed into Libya, and Africa's Great Rift Valley might sink farther to be flooded by seawater.

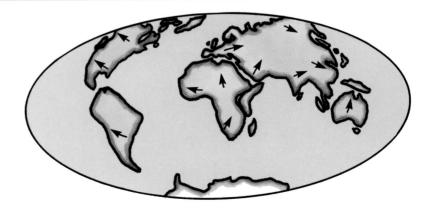

● **To the Parent**

The earth's interior consists of a superhot, solid inner core of iron, surrounded by a liquid outer iron core, and a mantle of superhot rock whose outer layer is partly molten. Floating on the mantle is the outer crust, formed of oceans and continents, which encases the earth like a shell.

❓ How Are the Great Lakes Linked to the Atlantic Ocean?

ANSWER Together, the Great Lakes are the world's largest body of fresh water. The five lakes between the United States and Canada are: Superior, Michigan, Huron, Erie, and Ontario. The lakes form a waterway from Lake Superior to Lake Ontario, which links the St. Lawrence River to the Atlantic.

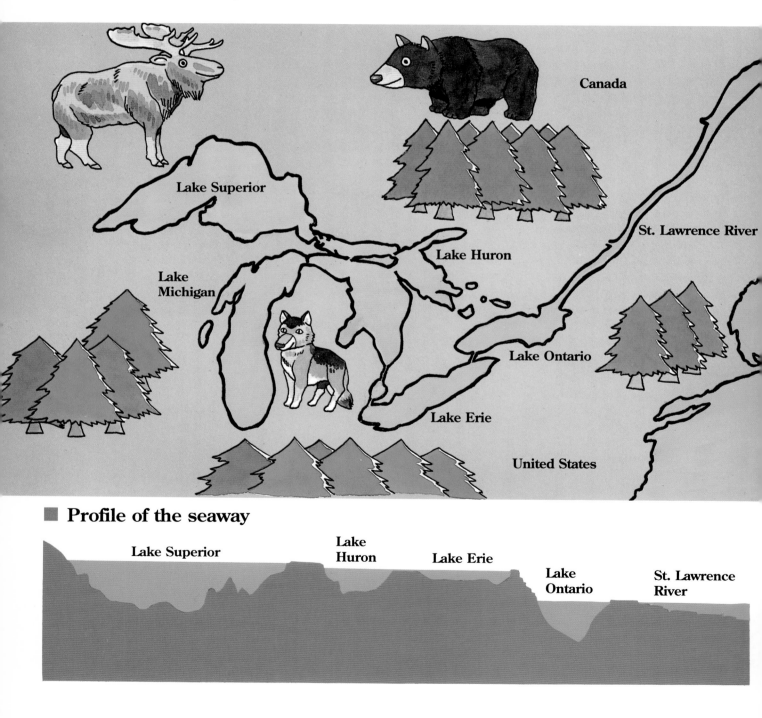

Canada

Lake Superior

St. Lawrence River

Lake Huron

Lake Michigan

Lake Ontario

Lake Erie

United States

■ Profile of the seaway

Lake Superior

Lake Huron

Lake Erie

Lake Ontario

St. Lawrence River

Can ships get through?

To even out the difference in elevation, ships are raised or lowered in locks *(right, top to bottom)*. Once the lock's gate closes behind the ship, the gate in front opens slightly to let the water level sink to that of the lower portion of the lake. When the water level inside the lock matches the lower level outside, the gate opens to let the ship pass.

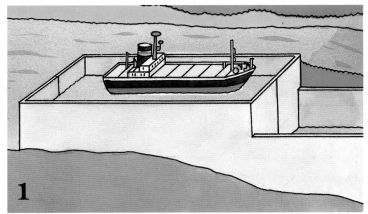

1

A ship enters a lock, which is a closed chamber with a gate at each end.

2

Water is pumped out of the lock to lower the water level to that of the next lake or canal.

Atlantic Ocean

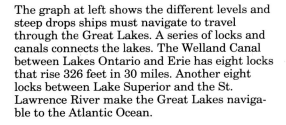

3

The gate opens and the ship enters the next lake, or in a series of locks, the next lock.

The graph at left shows the different levels and steep drops ships must navigate to travel through the Great Lakes. A series of locks and canals connects the lakes. The Welland Canal between Lakes Ontario and Erie has eight locks that rise 326 feet in 30 miles. Another eight locks between Lake Superior and the St. Lawrence River make the Great Lakes navigable to the Atlantic Ocean.

? How Are Artificial Lakes Made?

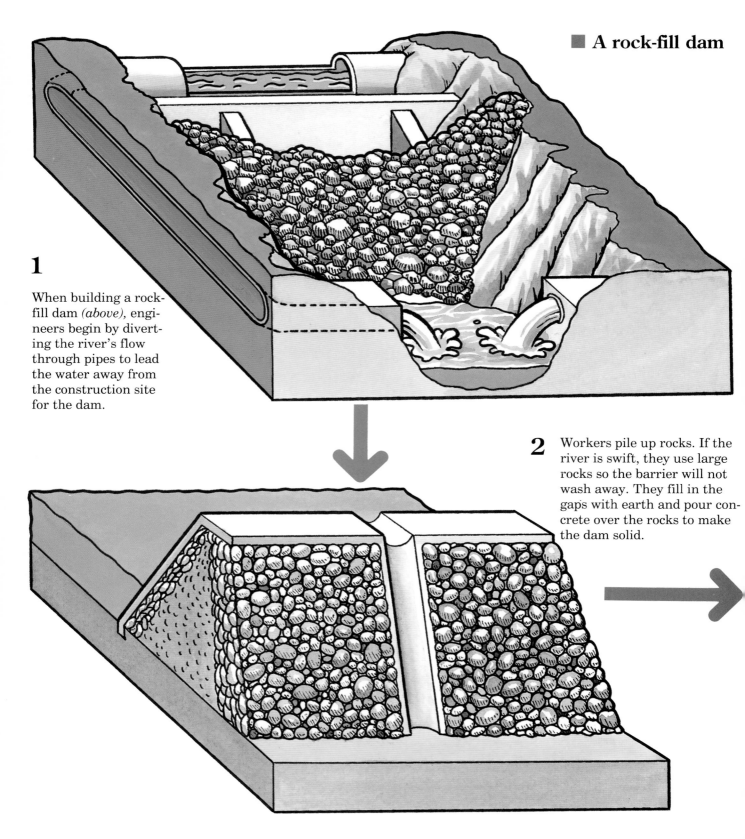

■ A rock-fill dam

1

When building a rock-fill dam *(above)*, engineers begin by diverting the river's flow through pipes to lead the water away from the construction site for the dam.

2 Workers pile up rocks. If the river is swift, they use large rocks so the barrier will not wash away. They fill in the gaps with earth and pour concrete over the rocks to make the dam solid.

ANSWER Artificial lakes are built by damming up a river. Of the two major types of dams, an arch dam curves upstream so that the force of the water pushes to the sides against the canyon walls. A gravity dam is built of rock and concrete holding back the water with its weight.

■ Two kinds of dams

▲ An arch dam

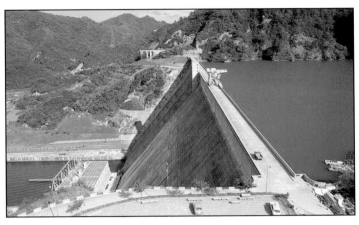

▲ A gravity dam

3

The finished dam is holding back the water with its massive weight. Spillways on the sides release excess water. Rock-fill dams like the one shown here are the oldest type of dam.

● To the Parent

Dams are built to make artificial lakes. The main use for these lakes is to generate electric power and supply water for homes or industrial use. Dams also serve in irrigation and aid in flood control. Dams may be built by a variety of construction methods, each developed to take account of differences in the width of rivers, the terrain surrounding each river, and the riverbed geology.

What Are the Biggest Landmasses in the World?

ANSWER The earth's landmasses are divided among seven continents: Europe and Asia, North and South America, Africa, Australia, and Antarctica.

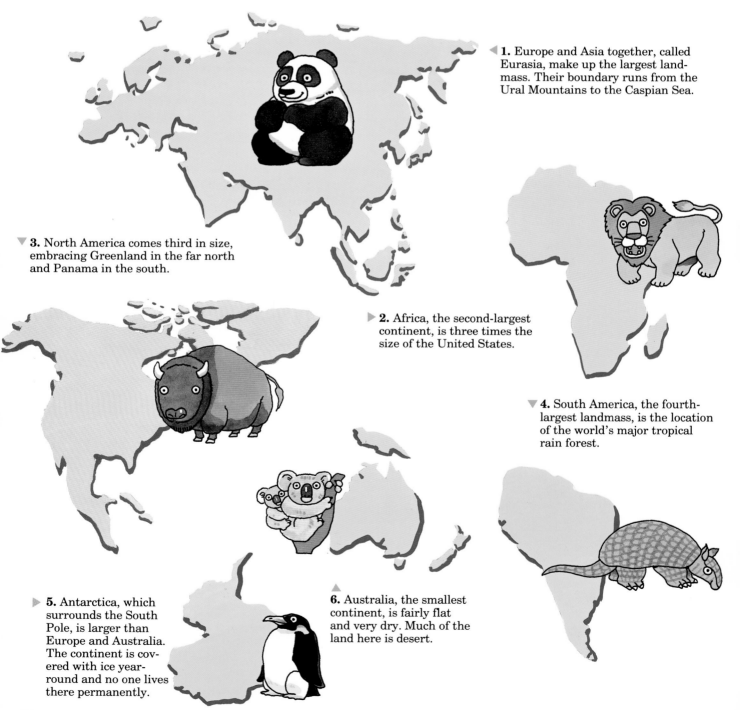

1. Europe and Asia together, called Eurasia, make up the largest landmass. Their boundary runs from the Ural Mountains to the Caspian Sea.

3. North America comes third in size, embracing Greenland in the far north and Panama in the south.

2. Africa, the second-largest continent, is three times the size of the United States.

4. South America, the fourth-largest landmass, is the location of the world's major tropical rain forest.

5. Antarctica, which surrounds the South Pole, is larger than Europe and Australia. The continent is covered with ice year-round and no one lives there permanently.

6. Australia, the smallest continent, is fairly flat and very dry. Much of the land here is desert.

What about big islands?

Greenland, the largest island in the world, lies off the northeast coast of Canada. Although much of the land is icebound year-round, about 55,000 people live there.

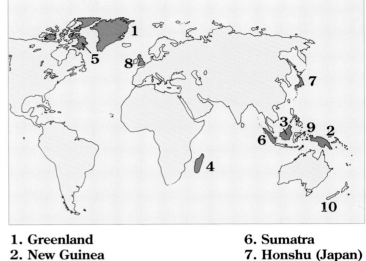

1. Greenland
2. New Guinea
3. Borneo
4. Madagascar
5. Baffin Island

6. Sumatra
7. Honshu (Japan)
8. Great Britain
9. Celebes
10. New Zealand South Island

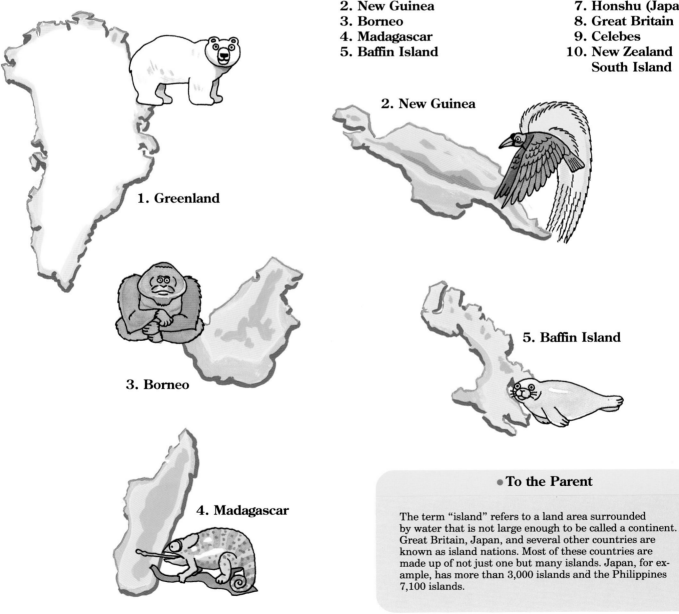

1. Greenland

2. New Guinea

3. Borneo

4. Madagascar

5. Baffin Island

●To the Parent

The term "island" refers to a land area surrounded by water that is not large enough to be called a continent. Great Britain, Japan, and several other countries are known as island nations. Most of these countries are made up of not just one but many islands. Japan, for example, has more than 3,000 islands and the Philippines 7,100 islands.

? Are Fish Caught All over the Ocean?

ANSWER Fish swim in all the oceans. To catch the most fish, fishing companies send their boats where they can find a lot of fish in one place. Fish like to gather where the water is not too cold and not too warm and where there is plenty of plankton for them to eat. Fishermen know about these gathering places and seek them out to get the best catch.

3. Off U.S. East Coast

Cod, herring, and flounder, as well as shellfish are the main catch in the eastern coastal waters.

4. Near Morocco

Herring, along with other fish, are also caught in African waters.

■ Fishing grounds

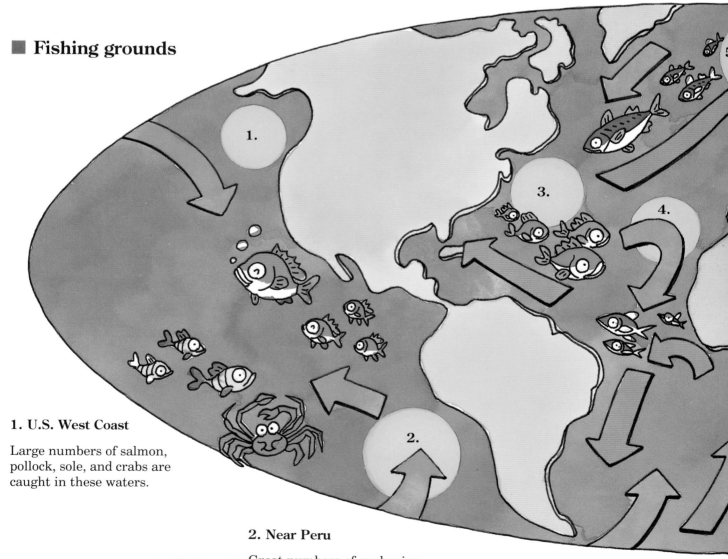

1. U.S. West Coast

Large numbers of salmon, pollock, sole, and crabs are caught in these waters.

2. Near Peru

Great numbers of anchovies, hake, mackerel, and sardines are taken from the coastal current.

■ Continental shelf

A continental shelf is shallow, allowing sunlight to reach the bottom and warm the currents. The water contains many nutrients, and seaweed can grow abundantly. This plentiful food attracts many fish, making the area an ideal fishing ground.

5. Near England

Large hauls of herring, mackerel, and tuna are the typical catch here.

6. Near the Philippines

Tuna and bonito, as well as shrimp, are taken from these waters.

7. Near Japan

These seas are rich in sardines, bonito, and many other kinds of fish.

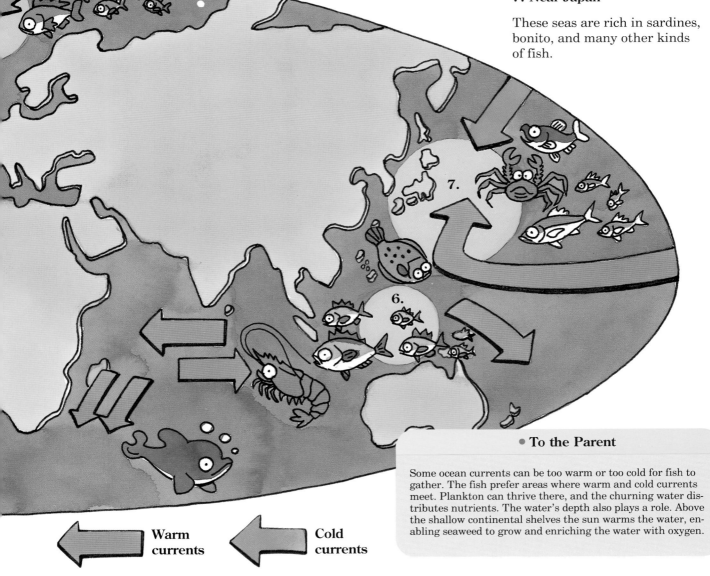

Warm currents

Cold currents

● To the Parent

Some ocean currents can be too warm or too cold for fish to gather. The fish prefer areas where warm and cold currents meet. Plankton can thrive there, and the churning water distributes nutrients. The water's depth also plays a role. Above the shallow continental shelves the sun warms the water, enabling seaweed to grow and enriching the water with oxygen.

Are Gold and Diamonds Found in Every Country?

ANSWER Gold is found in many countries; it is washed up in rivers or dug from deep underground. Only a few countries have diamond deposits. The major sites for each are shown below. At right, a miner digs deeper into a shaft to reach precious minerals.

The World's Largest Deposits

Russia

3.

2.

1.

2.

Zaire

1.

Namibia   Botswana

South
Africa

5.

4.

Australia

Gold

Diamonds

5.

United States

3.

4.

● To the Parent

Gold has been mined since prehistoric times and was probably the first metal used by humans. What makes gold so attractive is that it can be found as pure metal and does not require complex separating techniques. It is so soft that it can easily be worked into jewelry. Gold deposits exist in the form of grains in sand or gravel, or as veins in rock. Diamonds, looking much like pebbles when they are mined, begin to sparkle only when they are cut and polished.

❓ How Are Maps Different?

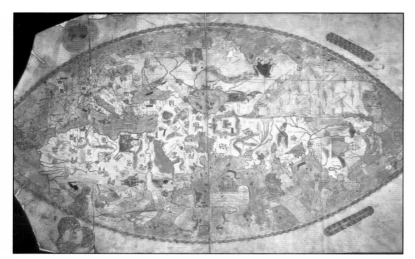

■ An old map

The ancient world map at left was drawn in Genoa, Italy, in 1457. The map shows Europe and parts of Africa and Asia. How does this map compare with modern maps of the world?

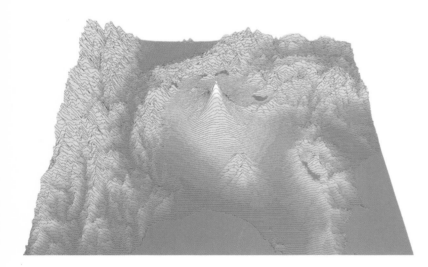

■ A computer map

The modern computer map at left shows mountains and valleys, giving a three-dimensional effect. The map can be rotated, to show how the land looks from different sides.

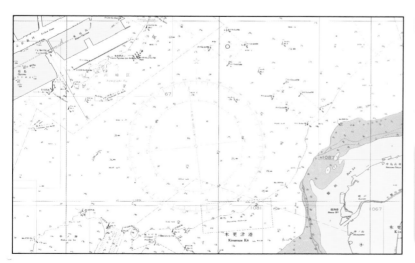

■ A maritime chart

The chart at left of Tokyo Bay, Japan, shows course bearings, water depth, obstacles, and other things a ship's captain needs to know to steer the ship safely through the water.

● To the Parent

Maps giving simple directions about a local area date back to at least 2300 BC, as clay tablets from ancient Babylon attest. The oldest known world map, also from Babylon, was drawn about 600 BC, showing Babylon at the center surrounded by the oceans. Only since the beginning of the 20th century have maps portrayed the earth accurately.

Growing-Up Album

Match the Pictures and Maps

Maps can show different landforms, roads, and cities. Which map matches which picture? Connect them with lines.

Mountains   A.

A port   B.

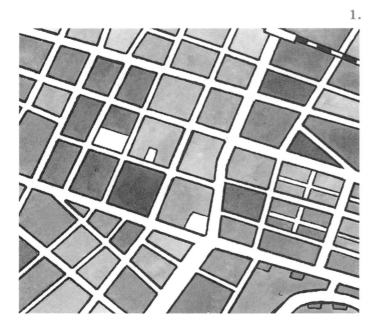

1.

2.

A town   C.

The earth   D.

3.

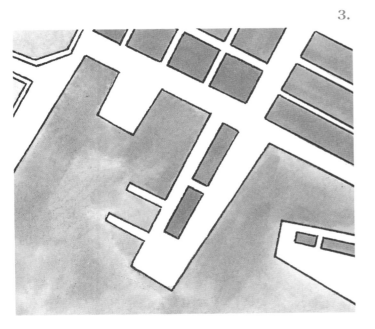

4.

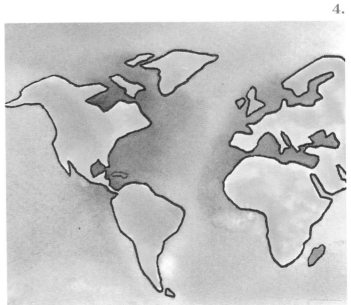

Match the Foods to the People Who Eat Them

A. Eskimo (North America)

B. Mexican (North America)

C. Englishman (Europe)

D. Guinean (Africa)

1. Rice

2. Bread

3. Yams

4. Noodles

The food that is eaten most of the time in any country is called a staple food. What is the staple food of the people who live in the countries marked (A) to (G)? Choose from the pictures numbered (1) to (7).

F. Chinese (East Asia)

G. Japanese (East Asia)

E. Saudi Arabian (Middle East)

5. Fish

6. Corn

7. Dates

Answers: (A)—(5); (B)—(6); (C)—(2); (D)—(3); (E)—(7); (F)—(4); (G)—(1).

Which Lake Is Larger?

The illustration below shows five of
the largest lakes in the world. Can
you arrange them in order of size?

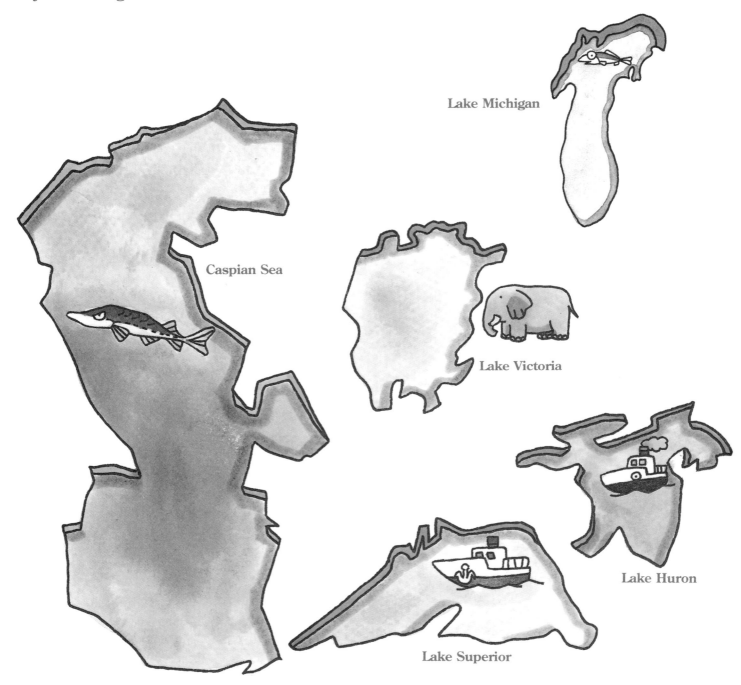

Lake Michigan

Caspian Sea

Lake Victoria

Lake Huron

Lake Superior

Answers: (1) Caspian Sea; (2) Lake Superior; (3) Lake Victoria; (4) Lake Huron; (5) Lake Michigan.

Match the Words and Pictures

A. Highest mountain

Some of the biggest places on earth are shown below. Name the mountain, river, ocean, or island and write the name in the box under each illustration.

B. Largest ocean

C. Longest river

D. Largest island

1. Nile River
2. Mount Everest
3. Greenland
4. Pacific Ocean

Answers: (A) Mount Everest; (B) Pacific Ocean; (C) Nile River; (D) Greenland.

A Child's First Library of Learning

Staff for
GEOGRAPHY

Editorial Director: Karin Kinney
Editorial Coordinator: Marike van der Veen
Editorial Assistant: Mary M. Saxton
Production Manager: Marlene Zack
Copyeditors: Barbara F. Quarmby (Senior), Heidi A. Fritschel
Picture Coordinator: David A. Herod
Production: Celia Beattie
Supervisor of Quality Control: James King
Assistant Supervisor of Quality Control: Miriam Newton
Library: Louise D. Forstall
Computer Composition: Deborah G. Tait (Manager),
    Monika D. Thayer, Janet Barnes Syring, Lillian Daniels

Design/Illustration: Antonio Alcalá, John Jackson,
    David Neal Wiseman
Photography/Illustration: 4 and 6: art by Yvette Watson; 23
    (top) and 26: art by Al Kettler; 55 *(left, top and bottom)*,
    64-65: art by Yvette Watson; 67: photo by QA Photo, Ltd.
Special Contributor: Barabara Beroth (research)
Overread: Barbara Klein

Library of Congress Cataloging-in-Publication Data
Geography.
    p.   cm. – (A Child's First Library of Learning)
    Summary: Through easy-to-read questions and answers,
    readers learn about maps of the world, and what they reveal
    about earth's people and resources. Includes charts,
    diagrams, and an activity section.
    ISBN 0-8094-9462-0
    ISBN 0-8094-9463-9 (lib. bdg.)
    1. Geography—Juvenile literature. [1. Geography—
    Miscellanea. 2. Questions and answers.] I. Series.
G133.G46 1994
910–dc20   93-28237
                                                   CIP
                                                    AC

TIME-LIFE for CHILDREN ®

Managing Editor: Patricia Daniels
Editorial Directors: Jean Burke Crawford, Allan Fallow,
    Karin Kinney, Sara Mark
Editorial Coordinator: Marike van der Veen
Editorial Assistant: Mary M. Saxton

Original English translation by International Editorial Services
Inc./C. E. Berry

First printing. Printed in U.S.A.
Published simultaneously in Canada.

Time Life Inc. is a wholly owned subsidiary of
THE TIME INC. BOOK COMPANY.

TIME LIFE is a trademark of Time Warner Inc. U.S.A.

School and library distribution by Time-Life Education,
P.O. Box 85026, Richmond, Virginia 23285-5026.
For subscription information, call 1-800-621-7026.